A RAT IN A TANK

Harry Gell

MINERVA PRESS
MONTREUX LONDON WASHINGTON

A RAT IN A TANK
Copyright © Harry Gell 1995

ISBN 1 85863 549 7

First published 1995 by
MINERVA PRESS
1 Cromwell Place
London SW7 2JE

Printed in Great Britain by
B.W.D. Ltd., Northolt, Middlesex

A RAT IN A TANK

FOREWORD

This record of one tank man's experiences during the second world war is not strictly a book of reminiscences, in the sense that I have recalled them from forty and more years ago. It is a record kept at the time or written immediately after the war had finished.

I kept a log on the journey out to the Middle East. I had also asked my family at home to keep my letters and when I finally got home, I wrote some sketches around a few of the personalities I had met and got to know.

I have pondered on how to present these three elements and decided that the least complicated way is the best.

Even though this way means no strict chronological order and a small amount of duplication, I feel that the experiences of a rat in a tank, more often than not day-to-day incidents and not very frequently the hurly-burly of battle, so presented reflect the life of a tank man first in the desert and then in Europe, Italy and the Second Front.

There is an admirable book, *The Sharpshooters at War*, by Andrew Graham, published in 1964, which gives a careful but very readable record of the actions where the regiment was involved and which would provide the battle background to these experiences. But fortunately for a fighting soldier's sanity, there are just as many experiences which are about anything but battle and it was those about which for the most part I told them at home. We could not say anything about any action in which we were involved until some time afterwards, usually at least a month, and therefore the incidents of battle come in later letters. I find, at this distance, that it is almost incredible that the one letter which was censored was dealt with as it was. I can only assume that it arrived in the hands of a very green young subaltern.

I have inserted from time to time the dates of the main events with which we are concerned. For those of my generation they will be relevant. But for anyone of the post-war years, and they are now the vast majority, I hope it may give them an idea of what life as a soldier was like and tell them that all was not blood, toil and tears.

And one last introductory word. These letters and sketches were written more than forty years ago and in the heat of the experience. I have wondered whether some passages should be included, those particularly recounting the atrocities which we came across. Reading them now, I realise that they are couched in unconciliatory language. At this distance I hope that they will not be taken as condemnatory or recriminatory of any nation, but of the practices and the vileness to which war leads ordinary people.

THE JOURNEY OUT
MAY - JUNE 1942

Thursday, May 7th., 1942

Arrived at Liverpool about 4 o'clock. It took an hour or so for us to get on board. In the meantime we were given a cup of tea from an army lorry which went along the length of the column. Eventually we got on board and found conditions at least as bad as the worst any of us had imagined. Talk about the Altmark and slave ships!

Our mess has 24 tables of 18 fellows in it - 432 if my arithmetic is correct. Its size is 80ft. by 80ft. and out of this come the staircase (companionway) and hatch. In this space everything must be done - eating and sleeping; and since the recreation room is so small that it is impossible for more than an infinitesimal minority of the men to get in it, the mess has to serve for recreation too.

Friday, May 8th.

We move a little down the river - to opposite Great Crosby. More revelations of the slave ship. To get any meal for the 18 men it takes three men to queue for anything over an hour each. This state exists very largely through the men's fault themselves. They are afraid that if they do not get into the food queue at 6 o'clock for 7.15 breakfast, for example, they might be a little late bringing the food back to the men. I am refusing to waste my time in that way. I will go to the queue about the time the meal is due and I may have to wait twenty minutes or so then. The gangways become almost impossible during these meal times, with queues on both sides and sometimes down the middle too and people trying to pass in both directions. Most of these are ship's crew or catering staff and the delay in getting the meals is greater.

Saturday, May 9th.

Still riding off the sand banks of the Mersey. Another extraordinary thing today. We are told it is our last opportunity to wash any clothes until we get to the first port. I have three pairs of socks, a vest and a towel to wash. During the morning it is absolutely hopeless to get anywhere near a washroom. Long queues (once again) form up at the few lavatories on board and fellows are waiting a couple of hours or more to do their smalls. I managed to get a bowl after only ten minutes' wait in the afternoon. Having finished the washing, I have to arrange it on the lines "fore and aft" and then sit and wait until it dries. It is not safe to leave anything for a minute. It amuses me very much to be sitting and reading a book until the socks dry. But it is a serious consideration that a crowded communal life, such as this on board a troopship, makes ordinary decent fellows forget the rights of private possessions and they are willing to filch anything from their comrades.

Sunday, May 10th.

We move about 4.30 in the afternoon. Rumour says it is only to Glasgow, where we meet the rest of the convoy. Rumour among the troops is about as fickle as it can be, however.

We have already received detailed courses to S. Africa, calling at Freetown on the twelfth day after joining the convoy, and Capetown or Durban - "This boat always calls at Durban" - on the 29th. But today we hear stories of a route via Iceland, Greenland, U.S.A., South America and Capetown. This convoy is also the largest troop movement ever undertaken, the fastest and the least protected.

A meeting of the entertainments committee this afternoon. It is self-appointed, I think. It is quite by chance I go and find myself the only representative of B Squadron. We make preliminary plans for concerts (talent competitions), boxing tournaments and a quiz, Regiment v 47th R.T.R.. I rake round and find eight or nine willing victims for the talent competition from the squadron.

I have not mentioned sleeping. The hammocks are slung absolutely as tight as possible. They are not only head to foot, but another line comes down between and so there is a head somewhere about one's knees. I am lucky in having a hammock at the very end of the mess, so that I have only a head at my feet and one on each side of my legs, not forgetting, of course, the fellow on each side of me, whom I knock every time I turn in the hammock. I have slept quite well, much to my surprise. I have not yet fallen out, although that experience will come, no doubt. It is comfortable to sleep in the hammock, as there is plenty of room and it is easy to turn in.

Monday, May 11th.

We join up with the convoy and really get going. Before breakfast, we are off the Clyde; Ailsa Craig the one landmark we can recognise. Then until early evening we see the Scottish coastline. It is beautiful and rugged. Sailing in convoy is in many ways strange, to see the same boat in relatively the same place every time one comes on deck, to realise that on each one of these sixteen or so boats there is a little world complete in itself as we on this boat are, and larger than many English villages spread over several hundred square miles. Ewhurst* for example, has far less in even the swollen wartime population, than has this ship, but its acreage was probably as large as the area covered by the whole of this convoy.

Tuesday, May 12th.

The sea, so far, has been extremely calm. It is amazing to think of the Atlantic as a mill-pond and yet that is what it has been so far. I am on guard all day - my job is to see that no troops go into the crew's quarters and to watch for fire. There is a very large guard here, 31 sentry posts, I think. Like all guards, though, it is there to prevent the one chance in a thousand. During the day I have the time to realise how insensitive I have become. The "last sight of England" and all that nostalgic rubbish just does not exist. I suppose I felt the shock of having to go abroad much earlier, when I realised that we were for the "high jump" and by the time the event had arrived, I had adjusted myself. Anyhow I have felt extremely phlegmatic since coming on board.

---

* A village in Surrey which I left to join the army.

Wednesday, May 13th.

I finish my last guard at 5 and have a hot sea-water shower. It is most refreshing. I think I must find enough energy to get up in time to have such a shower. I was walking round the deck at 6.30 and shortly afterwards, we were going through a long patch of oil. On it in one place was floating a sailor's emergency kit. Later in the day we hear that the destroyers in the convoy went off during the night on a submarine chase. I hope the oil meant the end of one - their life or ours, a primitive affair.

The escort seems to consist of seven destroyers, a light cruiser and an armed merchant cruiser. It is most interesting to see the escort change positions. Sometimes they must be five or more miles away; sometimes they seem to be just outside the convoy.

Towards evening it becomes choppy and a heavy mist comes down. The boat is still very steady though. Tonight the blackout is fifty-six minutes earlier than last night; that shows how far south we are getting.

Thursday, May 14th.

I am on fatigue today, helping the canteen staff. It is an eye-opener. We are supposed to be waging war for democracy and freedom, which implies, I suppose, the end of privilege. Yet the stuff we deliver this morning to the officers' mess; sherry, port, whiskey, gin and liqueurs, have been unobtainable for months in civvy street. I understand too that the casualties from sea-sickness among the officers have been much higher than among the troops, probably due to the high living that has been going on on the upper decks.

Towards evening it becomes much rougher and heavy rain begins. It is fascinating to watch the sea - it is always changing, never the same. I can watch it for hours.

Friday, May 15th.

Another day comes and goes. Time is passing very rapidly. Our daily routine is - up just after six and roll up hammocks, which must be out of the way, that is, stacked, by six forty-five. Then a shower; it is temporarily refreshing, but my clothes feel sticky still; that is because we have been sleeping in our clothes for the past three nights. We should be out of the danger zone in a day or two and then we can go to bed normally dressed.

Breakfast at seven-fifteen, but a walk round the deck before. All above decks by nine o'clock so that the mess orderlies can clear up the mess deck. A squadron roll call at nine o'clock. Then hanging about on the decks until a boat muster at eleven-thirty. As everyone is above decks, there is no room to sit down and read.

A very tiring period. The boat muster is usually at eleven-thirty, but sometimes it is postponed until four-thirty in the afternoon. We have to go first of all to action stations, then, on the alarm, to boat stations. From our mess, this is a slow process. We are a long way down and have only narrow corridors to go along. We are then normally free until lunch, but sometimes a lecture or P.T. is put in. Lunch is at one o'clock. We begin troop training again at two. This training consists of semaphore, the guns, Besa and Bren, tank tactics and the like. Tea is at six o'clock. Hammocks may be hung at eight. Lights out at nine-thirty. There is not a lot of time to oneself in this programme.

Saturday, May 16th.

We are now out of the really dangerous zone. We have lost five of the seven destroyers and the remaining two disappear during the day. The light cruiser and the armed merchant cruiser take up different positions; at one time of the evening they are at the extreme wings of the convoy - "left wing and right wing dribbling up the field" as some wit says. The atmosphere among the troops is much quieter. The "if" has now changed to "when", it's "when we arrive" now. The attitude has been very curious. There is still a nostalgia showing itself in such phrases as: "Shall it be the Sussex tonight?" or "What about seeing City play Wednesday this afternoon?"

Sunday, May 17th.

We seem to be approaching the tropics. The water is now a Reckitt's blue. I understand the term 'ultramarine blue' now. There have been a number of seaweed clumps like sponges floating just under the surface today. The sun is almost directly overhead, the first time I have experienced that.

The heat of the sun even through a cloud haze is too much and we have to move into the shade. We are playing bridge and have a good session, with a typical incident from the adjutant near the end. A couple of dozen officers had passed us squatting on the deck; the C.O. had watched a hand or two, but the kid of an adjutant said, as he passed by, "Keep out of the gangway." He is a first class worm.

The sunset produces a vast range of colours and a knife edge horizon. The fleecy clouds are mauve, the sun itself gold, and the reflection from the deep blue sea, silver (and deep does not refer to the number of fathoms).

The church service in the morning is short and enjoyable rather than inspiring. Ships' services always seem to hold a particular attraction, though. Perhaps it is only when faced by nature and nothing else that men see the place and even the existence of God.

Monday, May 18th.

The sea is even deeper today. It is a blue-black ink colour now. I see my first flying fish - very small and like a dragon fly and moving for a short distance at an extraordinary speed. We liven up the afternoon with a debate, "Should Church Parades be abolished?" The supporters of Church Parades were all non-church goers and the opposers all church goers. I think that those who supported genuinely realised that they were missing something but had not the courage or energy or initiative to go to Church of their own volition but needed a kick in the pants from the army to help them on their way.

Those who opposed realised that there was no need for compulsion and resented not being allowed to go of their own volition. Needless to say, the motion was defeated.

The debate was sponsored by Harrison, who is developing into a very decent officer. He is conscientious, fairly competent and easy to talk to, which is a quality I consider to be of paramount importance in an officer.

Tuesday, May 19th.

More flying fish today. One is as big as a whiting and flies for five yards or so, its wings being invisible. Some are much smaller, the size of sprats. These are the ones that look like dragonflies.

Our boat before breakfast has almost lost the convoy. It has apparently broken down during the night, but by taking a straight course instead of tacking with the convoy, it catches up again by mid-morning.

A talk today by Mays, on "Life in the army in India", a talk very much of the peacetime army given by a professional soldier. We civilians have little time or sympathy with such a life or views. We want to get the job done with as soon as possible and get back to our homes again.

The canvas awnings go out today, but it is not quite so hot and becomes quite chilly towards sunset.

The black-out is getting earlier and earlier - tonight it is at five past eight. There are more charges for smoking on deck after black-out; the punishment is seven days' field punishment.

Wednesday, May 21st.

Tonight I see phosphorescence for the first time. It is uncanny to watch the lights dart about and disappear, usually in one large flash. In a quiz this afternoon the explanation is given that these lights are really phosphorescent insects dashing hither and thither and finally being consumed by larger ones. I wonder if this is the correct solution.

The quiz is quite entertaining although Weston who runs it hasn't the first idea. He is a complete wash-out, it seems to me. If he can't organise things better in battle, I don't envy his troop.

The sleeping on deck has begun, so far it not being the turn of the troop. The absence of a fifth on deck has not appreciably altered the mess deck though. Some who say they cannot get to sleep, are not attempting to until after midnight which is disturbing for those who want to try. The journey is bringing all the worst out in the fellows. Selfishness is rampant and there is no consideration at all for the other fellow or his property. Things have got to alter before we get into battle.

Thursday, May 22nd.

The first meeting of the Discussion Circle. It achieves, I believe, what it sets out to do - be provocative and get people talking. To our surprise, 120 or more turn up. A number of casuals stop and listen and do not leave until it is finished. The subject is "The New Social Order" and many ideas come forward. Most is destructive criticism of the present state of affairs. The army is still decidedly red. We have to compete with a rival concert; the Brigadier and R.S.M. Jolly have arranged for tonight a series of sing-songs to which men are to be detailed. The O.C. Troops states that he has appointed an Entertainments Officer whose job is to do these things. In childish spite a voluntary and extemporary concert is held on the deck space next to the discussion. It will need men not children to win the war.

Friday, May 23rd.

We arrive at Freetown. Our introduction to equatorial Africa is romantic and fitting. The land appears as a pale blue silhouette just after breakfast. By ten o'clock it is fairly near and we are ordered to emergency stations, so that the ship may be stable while reaching her anchorage, which she does about twelve-thirty. We have been eleven days out of the sight of land. The coastline south of Freetown is quite mountainous. The slopes are covered with fairly thick scrub right down to the water, with coconut palms pushing through. The higher slopes are wooded. A number of valleys run down and split up the hills. There is a quaint little railway running up into the hills, a lighthouse at the harbour entrance, and great fuel tanks. I see and curse a building which looks like a badly designed factory from the Great West Road. It turns out to be a church.

As we are approaching the river, a couple of aircraft appear in front of us and A.A. fire comes up from the cruiser, apparently driving them off. If these are enemy or neutral planes, they are very smart on the spot.

A tanker draws up and we begin to take on fuel. Most of the crew are niggers, real dark Negroes. There are some beautifully built ones. They sing (in quite good English) and play antics for pennies which the fellows throw down on to the deck. They are very cute cadgers.

Saturday, May 24th.

I slept on deck and had a very comfortable night in spite of the hard boards.

There is a typical tropical thunderstorm hanging about most of the night and breaking about five o'clock. There are sheets of lightning like summer lightning at home but they seem to originate in balls of the same colour as the forks at home. There is no thunder. When the rain comes, it comes suddenly and terrifically heavily.

There is more gunfire this morning. It is practice from the shore-based batteries. So much for yesterday's scare, fanned by the Brigadier.

We hold a Whist Drive in the afternoon. Quite successful but we learn a number of lessons.

Black-out restrictions are relaxed while we are in port; it is strange once again after nearly three years, to see lights. Some of the ships look as if they are on a peacetime cruise. There are plenty of lights on the shore. The whole scene under the moon looks quite romantic, with the tropical moon - and I think many of us feel it too. I bet the folks at home have little idea that we are in tropical Africa tonight.

Sunday, May 25th.

A free day. I go to the O.D. (horrible name) service which includes an excellent address by Padre Lewis. The services are all crowded, which shows that a voluntary system of Church Parades is much more satisfactory.

The scrub or growth on shore looks very brilliant this morning. It is viridian green, seeming almost unreal, according to our standard of natural colours. The banks at the edge of the harbour are of red rock - I don't know what this really is. The harbour itself is a perfect, natural harbour, wide and seemingly deep. Some fellows go rowing in one of the ship's lifeboats. It is hot work for them, too hot for me even to volunteer, and they come back saturated. They almost seem to have been in a tropical storm.

Monday, May 26th.

A second discussion on "What is wrong with present day education?" It brings better speeches on the whole than the previous week. Once again there is a good deal of destructive and very little constructive criticism. We must attempt to make these discussions more constructive.

A storm breaks out towards the end of the discussion, a sudden howling of wind, rain in sheets and lightning, this time accompanied by thunder. The wind was a very strange, new experience. It was as violent as a gale at home, but was soft and warm and therefore pleasant to stand in.

Our training hours are now altered to give us an afternoon siesta period. During one we discussed the sun compass and the Sergeant Major gets tied up. Incidentally, he is very good at instruction. He comes back to clear up the point at two o'clock and afterwards becomes human. I think he must realise that he can get more out of the men by knowing them.

Tuesday, May 27th.

There are numerous canoes on the water here. They are obviously hewn from a tree, and are very skilfully balanced. The paddle is in the shape of a playing card spade. The natives are very skilful at manoeuvring these canoes. I see one crawl along his canoe, take a box, a large sugar box or something floating on the water, get it balanced on the canoe, and paddle off.

We leave Freetown about two o'clock. It takes a much shorter time to get out to sea than to get into port. The convoy seems to have formed up in no time and is properly under way again.

Wednesday, May 28th.

We are travelling at a good speed today. I sleep again on deck and sleep very well. Our "Book Exchange Bureau" is now working very comfortably. We (three of us who initiated the scheme) have a table with books on it. The fellows simply bring their books along and swap. It is a very easy system to work as no booking is necessary. We only have to keep our eye open to see that those books which are brought in are in a decent condition.

Thursday, May 29th.

We cross the Equator about one o'clock. The weather has been getting much pleasanter since we left Freetown. The sticky heat has gone and actually, as we were crossing the line, a very pleasant breeze was blowing. It has not been oppressively hot all day. The ship's news tells us that Rommel has started his offensive.

Sunday, May 31st.

A day spent on T.E.C. work (Troops Entertainment Committee). The morning is given up to the Book Exchange Bureau and then to the knock-out darts tournament. This was very popular and took about two and a half hours to get through. The afternoon saw a bridge drive. I had to help M.C. it, although I had little idea of how a bridge drive was run. Anyhow, after the first two hands, things ran smoothly.

It is a good thing that bridge attracts a good type of chap, or otherwise there might have been some unpleasant incidents. I hesitate to think what might have happened if the Whist Drive had hung fire quite so long last Saturday.

In the evening I play bridge myself and have a good rubber or two, which is enjoyable if not successful.

Monday, June lst.

Another day on guard. I find myself posted at the bottom of the stairs leading to the bridge and opposite the room of the O.C. Troops - quite entertaining. At dinner time for example, he has a nurse in for a pre-lunch drink, gin and lime by the look of it. The guard passes uneventfully. In the night my turn is when the moon is hiding behind the clouds and popping out just occasionally.

There are some beautiful effects with light silver patches on the water. Sometimes these are almost as far as one can see. It gets colder today and we put away our topees for berets. My best beret has been stolen. I must watch out for it on parade.

Tuesday, June 2nd.

I see my beret on parade this morning and having claimed it, get it back without a murmur. I try to trace what happened to it, but can get no satisfactory solution. Fellows are obviously not going to give themselves away.

Sleeping on deck is getting a risky business now. Once during the night my top blanket is blown right off me. The breeze, though strong, is quite pleasant.

And here for some reason the log stops. It is probably because the rest has been lost in the more than forty years since it was written. It is a pity because the remainder of the voyage to the Middle East had some interesting moments.

The ship broke down as we limped into Capetown. We waited there for eight days for another to take us on. The rest of the convoy left and we spent most of each day on shore.

I remember waiting in Adderley Street for a bus to take us to Table Mountain. When one came along and we moved forward to get on, a hand came on my shoulder and a typical South African lady said,

"Not on that bus George. (They called the British soldier George, not Tommy) That is for coloureds only."

That was my first experience of apartheid and the nausea which the incident caused was not washed away by seeing separate coaches for Europeans and non-Europeans on the suburban railways.

We went on a route march one morning to give us some exercise and we went, I fancy by mistake, through a shanty town. Again it was our first experience of anything like that, with rows of shacks built of anything, many of the flimsy petrol tins filled with earth and piled one on top of another for walls and covered with any bit of matting that could be found.

There was another incident which could have been nasty. We had one or two coloured men in the Brigade, and when one had tried to get into a cinema and been refused admission, the white soldiers in the audience were called out in protest.

But the letters home begin at this time and as they pick up the story of Capetown and Port Elizabeth, I leave them to tell the story of the rest of the voyage.

15. 6. 42.

We have just had a marvellous leave period. Through force of circumstances, which we don't pretend to understand, we have had longer at the port than most convoys. Unfortunately, after three severe winters at home with numerous records broken, we have met a record winter here - but it is daft to call it winter. We have had much more rain than is usual at this time of the year, four and a half inches in twenty-four hours at one time. Still, in spite of that we enjoyed ourselves tremendously; it really felt like being on holiday, and reminded me a lot of our jaunts round the continent.

I think we managed all this because the people welcomed us so heartily. It is difficult to describe how good they have been to us.

One afternoon a lady stopped us in the street and asked us if we would like to have tea with her. She took all five of us into a restaurant and as she was going, gave us her phone number in case we would like a ride. We phoned her up and she took us out - to three or four show places and then back for tea. After tea she excused herself, saying that she would have to be going as she was due at the hospital for an operation at five o'clock. You can imagine that that left us absolutely speechless. Think of giving up an afternoon before an operation to five complete strangers.

Another afternoon we were walking out in the country and a car overtook us. The fellow invited us to join him and took us down to a delightful little bay on the coast where we had tea. Then we went along the coast - most magnificent scenery, somewhat like Cornwall, but with mountains rising immediately behind the coastline. We passed on to the other side, and got a view of the next bay, which reminded me of pictures of Norway, and then back through forests and vineyards.

He also gave us his phone number and we spent an evening there just talking. He was a schoolmaster at the local secondary school and had visited England several times; so there was plenty to talk about.

Then yesterday he took us for another ride to another bay and another spot on the coast. Incidentally, I saw flamingos there in their natural setting. He planned another ride to one of the outstanding beauty spots in the world, but our time wouldn't allow it. He was just as disappointed as we were.

To add to the festivities, there was an opera week on, Aida and the Barber of Seville alternately with Eric's* orchestra accompanying them. I understand this is the first time that there has been opera for several years. It was partly amateur - chorus and ballet - but it was extremely good.

A lady sitting next to me was very nervous to know what I should think of it after seeing London shows, as she said. But it was really a very good performance.

The first night we went, we had boxes of chocolates passed to us from all the way round. Folk really did spoil us.

The local equivalent of the W.V.S. do an amazing piece of work too. They have information bureaux running, issue tickets for free travel on buses, fix up drives in private cars and run canteens in the suburbs and neighbourhood to which parties are taken out. There is tea there, and dances and supper too, I believe. I went one afternoon but spent most of the time stretched out on a boulder, asleep.

Well, we've started off on our journey again and left that behind us. Naturally we are all very sorry, but such things must be. Of course we don't know where we are bound.

---

* Eric Bray, of B.B.C. Orchestra.

5. 6. 42.

There seems to be another opportunity to get a letter off to you. Your mail doesn't seem to have caught up with us yet. I hope it does before long. I want to know very badly how you all are. I expect, at least I hope, that an airgraph we sent off a fortnight or more ago has got to you by now. Also that one letter we sent after a few days out has got home.

Since the last letter which I suppose I sent a fortnight or more ago, we have had another spell of shore leave. Once again we were very lucky. The people surely do know how to offer hospitality. I think each place must vie with the others to see who can make us most welcome.

Here we were walking along after having dinner in a hotel - we'd just come out as a matter of fact - when a lady and gentleman in a car drew up and invited us back to spend an evening with them. He was a motor salesman and importer, a partner in a firm here. His wife came from Welwyn Garden City. He was born out here, but we met his mother one night, and she was very Scotch.

Right at the end of the first evening we found that he was musical and that we liked music too. So the second evening we had a musical evening. He put on some records including the Cesar Frank Symphonic Variations for the piano. Do you remember Louis Kentner playing them at a B.B.C. lunchtime concert? It made me feel quite homesick.

A third night we went with the express purpose of having a bath. It was a great treat. We have had nothing but showers since leaving England.

They have a charming little daughter, just over two and a half. They had a film of her birthday party - quite amusing. We also saw films of the country a little bit further off than we have been able to get. They were grand films, in Technicolor, too.

Another night we went by a private hotel and were invited in to dinner once again. The proprietress's husband came from Northampton. I think he must have been a shoe operative and come over here to a shoe factory. He also knew S.E. London quite well - East Dulwich, Goose Green and that district particularly. The lady who invited us was going to church; so of course we joined her, although I would rather have stayed talking. I think you will hear from one or more of these folk we have met.

M.E.F. 16. 7. 42.

I hope you will have had an airgraph I sent off to you some days ago before you get this letter, the one I promised you in it. I believe an airgraph should get through in about ten days and an airmail letter in about three weeks, while ordinary correspondence will take I don't know how long. As I suggested in the airgraph, will you try these means too? You will see we have changed our address slightly and this may of course count for the delay in any mail getting to us.

I have waited to write until I found out what we could tell you. Apparently we can be a little more explicit about the journey now, but must leave you to guess where we are.

We were extremely lucky in the journey in more ways than one. Firstly, we saw no evidence of enemy activity at all. We must some time or other have come through submarine waters, but it was difficult to realise it. Everything was so peaceful and placid for most of the way. For days on end the sea was no rougher than Longholme*.

Secondly, we had very much more liberal shore leave than most fellows got. We had over a fortnight altogether. There is one crowd here who did not put a foot on dry land from the time they left until the time they arrived here.

Our first port of call was Freetown in Sierra Leone. We were there for several days but did not go ashore at all. It was quite a good introduction to Africa though.

The vegetation a very brilliant viridian green, fairly thick but not very high, with occasional date palms, (or coconuts, I don't know which) sticking through.

We saw little of the town itself as we were not opposite it, but it seemed strange to see buildings of obviously western construction and design planted down in vegetation of this kind.

Our next call was at Capetown. When we crossed the Equator it was fairly cool. We had no Neptune celebrations; I suppose there were too many of us. But we could buy a card saying that we had crossed the line and were therefore exempt from any further dues or ceremonies.

We got to within sight of land at the Cape as the sun was rising and I shall never forget the sight of Table Mountain against the

---

*at Bedford.

morning sky. It is supposed to be one of the sights of the world and I should certainly think it is.

As I have said in the letters I have sent since then, we had a marvellous reception there. If I were a resident, I think I should shut myself up when a convoy came in, but not they. Their hospitality was marvellous. It made me feel that much more might be done for the troops at home.

We heard Eric's orchestra accompanying opera while we were there. We made two sets of friends whom I have told you of before. The lady took us to Smuts' house, Kirstenbosch, the national gardens and the Rhodes memorial before going off to hospital. The schoolmaster took us further afield, to a little place called Camps Bay, and then along the sea road by the Twelve Apostles, twelve craggy mountains stretching for several miles along the coast, then through Constantia, the grape-growing part.

Another day we went to Muizenberg, a sea-side place on another bay, False Bay and a little place, Fishook, where we had tea. We saw flamingos there on the flats in their natural surroundings. They gave me quite a shock as flamingos always seemed ornamental birds for gardens before.

Capetown itself I thought a fine town. The buildings were those of a capital - Government House, Houses of Parliament, fine shopping centre and so on. I was surprised that Table Mountain was as near to the town. It seems to rise from immediately behind it. Unfortunately, the rains were on while we were there and we could not get to the top. The mountain railway was not open.

We went on from there to Port Elizabeth. This is a much smaller place, and more industrial. We had just as good luck in the people we met. We found them all most friendly and anxious to discuss things. The problems that interested us most were the colour bar and the subversive movement. It gave most of us a shock to see such a strong colour bar, different lavatories, different seats on the railway stations, different compartments, some buses for whites only, some for natives.

I must say that all the folk with whom we talked about it, did so very willingly and openly - although none seemed to have very strong reasons, apart from prejudice, for continuing the bar.

The subversive movement, they thought, was dying slowly now. It had been strong. It is called the Ossewa Brandewach, or O.B. for short, and definitely is out to help Mr. Hitler. Hence we had to be extremely careful in what we said even to the most friendly. We found that the loyal folk asked no questions about ships or our regiment or anything of that nature. There was plenty else to talk about.

Three things shook us up - the lights which I mentioned before, the fruit and the price of tobacco. I had more fruit in South Africa than I have ever had before in so short a time - oranges, apples, pineapples, guavas and figs mainly. There was fruit for every meal.

We went to one restaurant all the time, when we were eating out, and always finished with a fruit salad and ice-cream. There were plenty of eggs there, too.

Tobacco - I had a terrific shock when I asked for some cut plug and got a quarter pound for $1/1\frac{1}{2}$ - and quite good stuff too. The fellow at Port Elizabeth gave me a quarter for the boat, Government House, supposed to be the best S. African tobacco, 1/8 a quarter of a pound. On the second boat we were getting cigarettes at twenty for 4d.

We did the second half of the journey in another boat[*]. In many ways it had lots of advantages over the first. It had been, I should think, a luxury liner in peacetime. There was evidence of it; frescoes in the dining-hall, elaborate if garish decorations, a couple of swimming baths and so on.

It is quite exciting to go swimming. One day when we went, the boat was pitching a good deal and the water in the bath consequently went from one end to the other, so that I found myself swimming uphill.

I hope all goes well. I'm wondering what sort of weather you are having. I hardly expect you will have seen so much of the sun as we have in the last two months.

---

[*]The New Amsterdam.

THE MIDDLE EAST
JUNE 1942 - SEPTEMBER 1943

ALBERT

Don't please say "Albert" in the English way, but "Albere", for he was of French extraction. When we had completed our 20,000 miles round the Cape and had pitched our tents in the Suez Desert, he applied for privilege leave to go home. After Alamein, when we were back at Sidi Bishr, he found himself three miles from his parents. Lucky Albert.

He was, I believe, "in cotton," and had left Egypt to settle in Liverpool. He therefore found himself in the British army in this war and when he went abroad, he was going home. He became of course, our expert on all matters Egyptian. Within a day or two of arriving in Egypt, those of our troop in the tent were indulging in a "siesta" period, when the inevitable "chai wallah" came round. These two were from the Naffi institute on the camp site and had brought round with them an urn of tea. We found enough energy to take our mugs to the door of the tent, although Albert was still covered from head to foot and apparently asleep. We were still having difficulty with the money; we had not imprinted very firmly on our consciousness by that time that an "acker" or piastre was worth about 3d, nor did we recognise easily the value of coins. One of our number was going to pay for two mugs of tea at one acker each and offered a five acker piece. Some chatter went on between the Arabs and suddenly Albert jumped up, yelled at them "Tellala" and joined heatedly in the conversation. That incident has fixed firmly in my mind that "tellala" is three, as the Arabs were trying to give two ackers change and hoped that our inexperience would allow them a little quiet profit. Albert gave them as great a shock as he gave us.

He very seldom, however, used his Arabic. Soon, of course, we all picked up a few words and some became the most common words of the slang of the Eighth army.

"Maleesh" took the place of "San fairy Ann" or "ça ne fait rien" of the last war. The philosophy of "maleesh", "it doesn't matter", pervaded everything native in Egypt and soon had infected the troops too. "Mafeesh" was the "fini" and a most useful word when the Arabs came begging for "chai" or biscuits later in the campaign. "Couloo" meant the lot; "buss" alone; "sayeeda" good morning, good afternoon, goodnight or any form of greeting or farewell; "bint" a girl; "shufti" a look, and in military terms, reconnaissance; "kwayis," pronounced "quice" good; "muskwayis" bad, and "kwayis ketir" very good. Later in Italy, "bono" took the place of "kwayis"; "giorno" for "sayeeda" and "bambino" came into very common use.

A word in universal use among the troops is "wog." It refers to any native of the North Coast of Africa, whether Arab, Greek or Turk. I have tried to discover its origin for on one occasion I was told that it stood for Wily Oriental Gentleman. And as that explanation is as good as any other, I did not feel inclined to investigate any further.

While we were learning these words, we were also getting used to the life in the Middle East. Strangely enough, the heat did not try me most in those early weeks. Perhaps the Turkish baths we had experienced in the West Coast of Africa on the way out had made us impervious to the dry heat of the desert.

It was the dust and the flies that worried us most. The dust storms seemed to spring up every afternoon during those early weeks. The hot, dry wind would begin to blow and sweep in front of it the loose sand of the desert. Eddies of wind would build up a swirling column of sand a hundred feet high and if one's tent lay in the path of these, one knew all about it. The tent would billow and tug on the tent pegs, and anything loose would be caught in the whirlpool - I once saw a lilo bed sail upwards in the current - and when the column had passed, everything would be covered by sand. I suppose these afternoon phenomena were not real dust storms, not like one we had exactly a week before the Battle of Alamein.

That afternoon things began to happen about four o'clock. The sun turned a most peculiar colour, almost blood red and soon disappeared altogether. The dust was still high up though. An hour later the wind developed. It was almost impossible to keep our eyes open and the sand stung against our bare legs and faces. For three hours this wind-driven sand swept across the desert, looking very much like a blizzard on the Yorkshire moors. At eight o'clock I went across to the tank and with difficulty climbed into the turret. As I sat there I heard a curious clicking sound coming from the corner where the variometer of the wireless set was. It persisted and when I turned to look, I saw sparks from the variometer to the side of the tank; static electricity, I believe, is the scientific name for this display of nature.

I climbed out again and in the wind, went to steady myself by seizing the aerial, but a spark then flashed across the aerial and my hand.

I fought my way back to the little bivouac tent through the sand. It was beginning to rain then, large, even though infrequent spots. When I had crawled into the tent, though, it poured much more heavily.

There is not much room in one of these little bivouacs for two fellows and we were soon touching the walls, a most disastrous thing. The rain began to seep inside our tent and down on the sides of our blankets. The wind became stronger still and afraid of what it meant, we felt one of the tent pegs go. A second gone in the sand, and within a few minutes the whole tent had collapsed on top of us. No longer taut, it was no longer waterproof and cold streams trickled through on our faces. The storm seemed not in the least inclined to abate, and so heroically, after some twenty minutes, I decided I might as well get wet through, pitching the tent again. I clambered out, found a mallet and went round driving in the pegs. I stumbled before the wind, groping for boxes or petrol tins with which I could anchor the tent. I made a pretty good job of it, I flattered myself, and wet through to the skin, I crawled back into the bivvy. I stripped, an acrobatic feat to accomplish on one's back, with a tent that must not be touched, about one foot above one's head. I found something dry to put on and lay back. The din of the last few hours had gone. No howling and lashing now, only the softest patter of rain on the tent, and within five minutes that had ceased. I scrambled out for the last time that night, and found a beautiful starlit night. It was then half past nine.

The second nuisance was the flies. Army hygienic propaganda had warned us of these and told us how to avoid their worst dangers. Nothing could teach us how to save ourselves the irritation of having hundreds flying around and settling on us for eight or ten hours a day.

Whisks were no good, traps quite useless against such numbers, and although we might kill hundreds a day, it still seemed to make no impression on the millions left.

A large proportion of the fellows had within a few weeks of landing a particularly unpleasant disease which we called "gyppy tummy", a very expressive name. An attack would last for three or four days, and in a country where hot, sweet tea was needed as a thirst quencher, that same hot sweet tea was about the worst thing for gyppy tummy.

It was akin in many of its symptoms and results to dysentery and I wonder if that also were not fly-borne. I had one attack of it only and then I would have sworn that forty thousand little devils were chasing round my intestines.

These and the sand I never got used to, but the sights and sounds and smells of the near East soon became everyday experiences, and consequently, passed unnoticed.

I think that we all receive so many impressions of Egypt and Palestine from earliest Bible training that deep down in our consciousness, we know already what the country is like. It is all much too much like our preconceived ideas. The oases have their group of trees at the foot of the sand hills; the houses are made of the sun-dried mudbricks; the women wear their black robes from head to foot, and the men their white galabiehs. Camels are so universal a beast of burden that within a few days they pass unnoticed. The dhow is so much part of the scene, that even when a large W.D. is painted on one, it is unremarkable. One feature that never failed to amuse me was the common ass. He is small and so good tempered. He is used as a bicycle; in fact in Tripoli, the Arab on the bicycle and his brother on the ass are mixed up on the streets. The Arab sits on his back quarters, his legs dangling on either side and almost touching the ground. He will kick the poor beast with his heels when he wants him to speed up. And Arabs and ass thus jogging along are the commonest sight of the roads, whether in country or town.

The modes and methods of agriculture seem as primitive too as in Biblical times. The camel or cow pulls the wooden plough, which is really nothing more than a wedge of wood. Usually, one of the women of the household will be driving it. Sowing is of course by hand. Irrigation is along narrow and shallow channels from the well to the field. In the delta the water seemed to be raised by the lever method, with a long pole swivelling on a cross bar, but here the water was raised only a few feet from a large canal or the Nile itself. Further west, where wells were used, a cow pulled up the goat skin over a pulley. A sloping runway would be dug the length of the rope, so that the poor beast had a downhill pull when raising. The pulleys invariably squeaked and I heard that there were superstitions about this. It is true however, that on one occasion, when we were near some wells for several days, some of our fellows greased one of these pulleys that had been making the most hideous noise from half past three in the morning onwards, and promptly the family packed up, tents, mats, animals and everything and left. That is one great advantage of this nomadic life. If you don't like your new neighbours, you can pack everything and move the next morning. We caused quite a number of such migrations between the Delta and Tunis.

But all this is a very long way from Albert. He was essentially a man of the towns. He knew all the good bars in Alex and introduced us to them. He told me, for example, that at Atheneos, "You can buy cakes such as you have never tasted in your life before." This forecast was almost correct, too.

Atheneos is a most pleasant place for afternoon tea. The large room looks over the bay, and the cakes are delicious. There one goes round the trays in the shop, and selects what kind one wants. The bar itself was in the process of being spoilt, while I was there, by becoming very noisy and crowded.

I shall, however, remember Albert mostly as the fellow who travelled 20,000 miles for compassionate leave at home.

M.E.F. 27. 7. 42.

I was delighted to get your cable tonight. It's eleven weeks tomorrow since I last heard from you - or maybe it's twelve.

We are settling down here quite well. The sun, dust and flies are trying at times, but taking all in all we are not hurting. In point of fact we have been extremely lucky ever since we left England, but the reasons, I must keep to myself for the time being. At the moment we are spending the time training, or perhaps I should say re-training. We are gradually getting used to seeing perpetual sun. Yesterday was the first day when we saw any cloud at all after nine o'clock in the morning. The sky at night is marvellous. In the southern hemisphere we thought there must be many more stars in the sky than in the northern but here we can see thousands that are missing at home.

Dust and flies take more getting used to; the dust seems to come up each afternoon. Sometimes it comes in a whirlwind affair which reaches up two hundred feet or more in the air. It is not pleasant to be in the path of one of those. Flies are a pest, particularly as they carry so many germs. We kill as many as we can, but that's not enough.

I have twice been to the nearest town, some twenty miles off. I believe that Egypt could have some charm for you, but it would not hold much if you could see some parts of this place.

There is a canal running through and one bank of this is very pleasant. There are gardens with quite a variety of palms. Some have perfectly smooth bark. Then there is an avenue of "flame trees." The leaf is rather like the mountain ash, but it has a large flame-coloured flower. It is strange to see a tree of this size with so large a flower. There is a garden club for the forces here - a very pleasant place.

The Arab quarter, even that part "in bounds" has to be seen to be believed. We've all heard of hens walking in the front door and so on, but I'm afraid it needed the experience of seeing it to punch it right into my head. There was the dirty, filthy hen walking into the house from the street, a goat tethered to a post a yard from the front door, and all the garbage over the road, which had just been thrown from the front door.

The houses are plaster on reeds, or just mud. Yet in spite of this, there are some quite beautiful pictures. One I shall not forget is of a mosque in these quarters.

M.E.F. 2. 8. 42.

I had seven letters in the first batch; not bad, is it? And I can think of no better way of spending a Sunday afternoon 20,000 miles or so away from home, than on one's back in a tent in the desert, spending an hour and a half reading letters from home.

Yours were posted on May 13th, and 20th and 27th. I can assure you it doesn't make any difference how old the news in the letters is. It doesn't matter whether I read what you are doing this Sunday afternoon or a Sunday afternoon nine weeks ago. It is a curious state of mind, but a happy one.

I was called off for another issue of mail - another five letters for me, including yours of May 5th, which you thought I'd get before I left, and of June 3rd.

17. 9. 42.

We are in another spot in the desert again and it is not as flat as we have experienced most of the time before. It is quite a welcome sight to see a skyline that is not completely flat or dissolved into mirages, in the heat of the day. I have not noticed any mirage about here, but previously we saw ships and sea and heaven alone knows what, and sometimes it was only five hundred yards off.

We have also seen a certain amount of bird life here. They seem to be quite tame and are a species I have never seen before, with a crooked beak, spotted chest like a thrush and a tail that wags like a wag-tail. Heaven alone knows what they feed on. They seem to nest in holes in the sand, probably rat or lizard holes originally.

The desert rat is also a very tame little creature and not nearly as loathsome as the vermin at home. It is something like a squirrel, with longer hind legs than front, and sits up to eat. It has a long, thin tail, with the last two inches like a Kleenezi brush.

I think I told you that the Nile is now at flood height, of importance to Egypt. All the irrigation canals are full and just seeping through to low-lying strips alongside. Coming by some of these the other day, we saw birds in the swampy bits that looked like small herons - long legs and necks.

We are experimenting at the moment with a filter for water - a petrol can filled with layers of gravel and sand.

We get half a gallon of water a day for drinking and washing (that does not include cookhouse water for tea etc.). It is just enough for personal washing and as much drinking as one wants. We've managed to train ourselves not to drink anything at mealtimes. But we now want something to wash our clothes in and hence this filter. In theory, we should be able to put all our dirty water in and it come out clean enough for clothes washing - and drinking too, but we won't test it to that extent. We are now anxiously waiting till after tea when we have our bath (in half a mess tin of water), and then pour the resulting soup into the filter.

2. 10. 42.

I am actually writing this letter in the Toc H house at Cairo. I was told quite suddenly on Thursday evening that I could go for three days' leave on Friday (yesterday) with two others from our troop. We came here and with a bit of wangling, managed to find beds in the house, although officially, the house is full for the next month.

We came quite frankly on a sight-seeing holiday, and have managed quite a bit already. Yesterday we went round old Cairo and visited some of the mosques. The modern city of Cairo has been built up of three or four quite separate towns. Old Cairo is where the Arab quarters are now, and is round the Citadel. We got ourselves set up with a dragoman (or guide) and were very glad we had or we shouldn't have liked to go through some of the places without the protection of a fez with us. The Arabs could spoil any holiday here if we let them. They pester terribly in the streets. Sometimes all you can do is take the protection of a shop.

Anyhow, we saw the oldest mosque, El Alzar, I believe, and one of the most beautiful, the Sultan Mohammed Ali Mosque.

It was quite amazing in the mosque itself - very dark to begin with, but then our eyes got used to it, lit by the sun through amber and blue windows. The sheikh's pulpit and praying desk, as we should call them, were most elaborately decorated with gold on a green background, the dome very high - about one hundred and fifty feet or so - an enormous red carpet over the whole floor and about four hundred lamps hanging (not lit then).

We also saw the Blue Mosque, as everyone seems to know this and is expected to go. It is a very inferior production. It gets its name from the blue faience with which the upper half of the walls are glazed.

Today we have of course been to the Pyramids. We went with the same dragoman, one Mahmoud Mahommet Tony.

The Pyramids are really amazing. Just remember all you have ever been told about them and multiply it about ten times and still you won't exaggerate - 2,300,000 blocks, each two and a half tons for example, covering about fifteen acres, in the case of the large one. Actually there are seven pyramids in the group with the largest one; three are rather decrepit though, and have lost their shape completely.

Then you can see another group some twenty-five miles away across the desert at Sakkara. There must be another seven or eight there.

We went into the Great Pyramid and what a journey that was! For about forty yards in one place you are climbing up an incline of about a one in four gradient and through a tunnel about three feet square. Then, to get into the Queen's chamber, you have another three foot tunnel about twenty yards long, but flat, to crawl through. After that there is a climb up to the Great Gallery to the King's tomb with another couple of ducks under low stones. The chamber itself is in real granite of even greater blocks than the others.

Then of course we went round the temples and the Sphinx. There are a number of temples that have been recently excavated and the Sphinx was not completely opened up until 1936. The Sphinx is quite interesting, as is the Temple of the Valley next door, but loses a lot in comparison with the Pyramid.

LEN

This record has not been written in chronological order. I am now in Normandy and have just seen Len again after an interval of nearly two years. But it is of the Len of the early days in the desert that I am going to write.

He did not settle down to life in the desert as easily or as readily as most fellows. He was the sort of chap who was irked by the petty orders and restrictions of the army, who liked to say, "Aren't we fighting for Democracy?" when another of our freedoms went and who therefore was not likely to adapt himself quickly to a fresh life. He became "sun-happy". He was not, I am convinced, completely responsible for his actions, and it says much for the Army which he so vehemently decried, that it was very patient with him.

Soon after his worst outbreak, I found myself thrown together with him quite a lot. We were detached from our squadron to do a course and Len and I and two others led a very "detached" life. It was while we were in this training that I first saw the Pyramids. We moved from the Suez desert to that west of Cairo and passed through the city and Gizah and by the Pyramids. I don't know why, but it struck me as most incongruous to see a double-carriageway motor road, and trams between, leading right to the base of the Pyramids. The ancient and modern were well mixed.

"Right to the base" is not really correct. There is five or ten minutes' walk from the tram terminus to the Great Pyramid, but so huge is it that such a distance does not appear to exist. On this passing visit we just skirted the Pyramids and watched them disappear across the sand with the red glow of the setting sun reflected on them, as we turned to the desert track from Cairo to Alexandria.

Three weeks before Alamein, Len and I and Stan found ourselves in Cairo again. We had the three days' "desert leave", which flooded Cairo and Alex, and must have given Rommel to think that our offensive was much farther off. Three days does not sound long for a leave but it was most welcome then and in retrospect I am even more glad of it now, as it was the only opportunity I had of visiting Cairo.

We were quite unashamedly sightseers during these days. We were lucky enough to find beds in Talbot House, largely through some wangling, but spent relatively little time there. We went first of all to see some of the Mosques, the Mohammet Ali, the Blue Mosque and anything else in the native quarter that was handy. We came across a dragoman quite by chance and allowed him to take us round. I say "quite by chance," as in the first place, probably with an eye to business no doubt, Tony came to our rescue with some shoeblacks. At this time these street boys were a pest in Cairo. They would follow soldiers about, worrying them, and if the soldier persisted in saying "no", they would throw some of their boot polish over his feet, ankles or trousers, as luck would have it, and then attempt to charge for cleaning it up.

I could never make out why the authorities did nothing to stop this abuse.

The Egyptian government under Nahas Pasha professed friendly relations towards the British and at least said that the British army had saved Cairo and the Delta from a German and Italian invasion, but they did nothing to ameliorate relations. They allowed the most flagrant profiteering and apparently turned a blind eye, at the other end of the social scale, to these guttersnipes. The pest was so serious that many British soldiers would not take leave in Cairo, or if there, would not walk along the streets and certainly on our third day we three hardly felt able to cope with the street nuisances.

But Tony, the dragoman, protected us while we were doing our sight-seeing. The Blue Mosque turned out to be a very second-rate affair. It is quite small and the blue tiles in the courtyard, from which it gets its name, are not by any means outstanding. But for some reason or another it has its glamour. The two things that I shall always remember though, are the interior of the Mohammet Ali Mosque and the city sounds from the Citadel. The Mohammet Ali Mosque is enormous and the actual Mosque most elaborately decorated. There is an enormous crimson carpet on the ground, and the praying desk is of light green and gold picking out quite complicated designs, and an enormous chandelier hangs from the centre. To me this Mosque, much more than the Blue Mosque, captured the lavishness of the East.

Then there was the view and the noise from the Citadel. Looking across the old city to the Pyramids, it is a typically Egyptian one, of crowded streets with here and there, palms. But the clamour that arose; bells, voices, particularly the high-pitched screaming of children, the braying of asses and the general bustle of a busy city, all combined to produce an audible atmosphere that no sound track from Hollywood could possibly capture.

Cairo in no way disappointed me. Even the modern streets had all the flavour of the near East. The Turkish Arabs, very respectable in their neat suits and tarbushes, mingled with the French and Greek, whose influence is still great in Egypt. The French and Greek women moreover, were as smart as their European sisters. The shop windows were well filled but had an oriental tang; perhaps it was a roll of camel-hair cloth in a tailor's window, perhaps an oriental café mixed up with American bars, perhaps it was the wog at an American bar smoking a hookah, a most elaborate affair in Egypt.

The near-East was there, helped by all the other near-eastern street characteristics such as the ubiquitous gharry, the porter at the gate of the large house in smart white galabieh and red sash, and that same accursed shoe-black.

Then through the middle of Cairo runs the Nile. It is all that school books have led us to believe, a dirty, swirling torrent, three or four times the width of the Thames at Westminster. The banks are not particularly beautiful. Occasionally there is a decent vista, as of St. George's Cathedral, or of the Gezirah Sporting Club opposite. But the riverside buildings compare much more with Southwark than with the Victoria Embankment.

And last of all there are the Pyramids. Prepared to be disappointed, we felt we could hardly return from Egypt without seeing the Pyramids. But I must confess I was in no way let down; I got all the thrill I had expected and perhaps a little more. Of course, the first thing that amazed me was the height, and the second thing, on approaching the Great Pyramid, was the size of each individual block. It is all very well to read that the height of the Great Pyramid is so many feet, the weight of each block so many tons, but all these facts mean nothing until one has seen it for oneself. All the time I was abroad, I think that this realisation that it needs actual experience really to make one appreciate a fact, was the one reality that kept imprinting itself on my mind. I wonder too quite what I, as a schoolmaster, can therefore really do. I had read in a book many a time, about the sun being overhead at the Equator and one's shadow disappearing into a small dark pool around one's feet, and I have trotted this fact out in a schoolroom, but of what use is this method of communicating in reality? And of what use are facts so communicated?

As with the Sun at the Equator, so with the Pyramids. All I had read or heard about them, needed a visit to really make an impression on my mind. I don't however, remember reading about the inside passages to the burial chambers - except in prophetic pamphlets. The crawling and climbing through dark and narrow corridors was an experience. Our dragoman bought candles which we each held and these, with others carried by more sight-seers, were all the light to grovel by inside.

Most of the passages were steep and were only about four feet square. Another, on the other hand, the main way into the burial chamber, I believe, was so lofty that our miserable candles could not penetrate to the roof. Then eventually the large room for the Pharaoh and the smaller one for his queen. Was it worth the climb? I doubt it, but at least I have experienced the inside of the Pyramid. And how I knew it when eventually we regained the sunlight. My khaki drill was wringing wet and even the heat of the sun seemed pleasant coolness.

Then a walk to the other ruins, the Temple of the Sun, the smaller Pyramids and the Sphinx. I was most surprised that, in contrast to the Pyramids, the Sphinx was much smaller than I had imagined. The photographs which show Pyramid and Sphinx as almost the same size must be taken from an artful angle. Really, the Sphinx is a midget compared to the Great Pyramid which looms away behind it in the distance. From the depth of the excavation, the Sphinx must have been well covered by the sand through the centuries. It is ridiculous, but my chief recollection of the Sphinx is the bit of his nose that was knocked off by one of Napoleon's cannon balls.

But our visit to Cairo was not only concerned with Mosques and Pyramids. We saw a Maskelyne show, almost exactly the same as I had seen at New Cross Empire some time before, but in what different surroundings! Instead of the warm, red plush and garish lights of a London variety hall, there was the cool blue sky above, such a depth of blue in it too, studded with stars, far, far more numerous than ever in London, and tall palms around the auditorium. It was when the line still stood at Alamein and when the Delta was still jittery about air raids which were of course more than a possibility from Crete and Greece.

The spotlights on the stage, therefore, could not compete with the powerful searchlights which criss-crossed the deep sky with their silver lattice half-way through the performance. However romantic such an atmosphere might seem to the fans of Ruby M. Ayres, I am pretty certain that I prefer the homely air of Deptford Broadway.

On a second night the three of us saw a Judy Canova film, at the Metro. Once again, a semi-oriental cinema was a new experience for us. We wondered why the chairs were of wicker, but we discovered that even wicker chairs will harbour fleas and I should hesitate to imagine what would happen in plush "fauteuils." In parenthesis, I might add that I was only bitten about three times by vermin and on each occasion it was in a theatre or cinema. I never collected them in my bedding or clothes and I firmly believe that such was the experience of most fellows. The cleanliness of the desert air and sand had much to be said for it.

Lastly we visited the Gezirah Sporting Club. An Englishman always wants to imagine he is still in England even if he is at the far ends of the earth, and Gezirah is the English corner of Cairo. On an island in the Nile, really, it is approached through gardens of cactus and palms, but inside, its grounds are laid out with much more subdued trees and roses. Then the Tennis courts, the Rugby pitch, the race course and the Cricket field all give a concentrated impression of England.

And as we three sat and watched the last cricket match of the season, I could appreciate how welcome such a corner is to any English exile, even though he has taken up residence in Egypt voluntarily.

Too soon the three days had gone and Len and Stan and I had to return to the desert. We were soon to launch upon the intensive X Corps training, but the three of us had seen something of Cairo and enjoyed our brief glimpses in each other's company.

15. 10. 42.

I've got your letter with the £2.2 in it. I've handed that in this morning to be changed. Our procedure is to give it in to the Squadron office; from there it is sent back to an Army Post Office somewhere and the hard cash comes out to us. We are getting 102½ piastres to the pound. The rate of exchange is somewhere about 97½ pt. So I will leave you to work out how much is lost in brokerage. Now I have just over £4 and will be well set up for several months ahead.

Not that we need much money in the desert. It mostly goes on tins of fruit, sweets and chocolate. The chocolate we get now is Egyptian and not too bad. It is rather like Aero, porous to look at. We have been quite well off the last week or two. We also lay by a little stock of tinned stuff for when we are on the move.

When we are moving, the tank crew cooks for itself. We carry a cooker with us - a variation of the Primus stove, and we also use what wood we can find; not much round here, although we came across some dead scrubby wood the other day. The tinned stuff that we buy, we use to supplement our issue food, beans with the bacon at breakfast, soup before the evening meal and so on. The other night I made the blokes a glorious Irish stew with a tin of soup as a basis, a tin of bully, another of peas and a fourth of tomatoes. Believe me, it was one of the tastiest meals I've had for a long time. All that is in answer really to your question of what the food is like. I miss fish and chips and regret not having new potatoes, green peas, strawberries and the other things I might have had if I had been in England, but really we do surprisingly well. Everything, including water, has to be brought to us miles across the desert, of course.

By the way, when I was in Cairo, I had fresh dates and figs. The dates were lovely, nice and golden in colour. The figs I did not like nearly as much as when dried. Raw they were rather tasteless, but stewed they had more body.

One of the "we" I've talked about as going to Cairo together is Stan Edwards who came with me to the regiment from Catterick and whom I've got to know quite well. He comes from Liverpool, is a wholesale fruit salesman, (at Sheffield actually when he was called up), is about thirty-five and has a girl of three. He has a very strange humour which comes out in very witty little sayings - as bluff and hearty as anyone can be.

The other is Len Williams, a young railway clerk from Crewe. He and I have been thrown together a good deal in the last months and I've got to know him well. He was then suffering from what we know as "sunhappy". The condition had got him down properly and he had done one period of C.B. since he has been here. But he has improved greatly now, and forgets the uncomfortable surroundings and interests himself in the work. He is quite a changed fellow. Bish is in another troop now and I don't see an awful lot of him, although he crept into our bivvy last night and we talked of kings and cabbages for an hour or so. He is the Oxford undergraduate from Guildford I picked up at Catterick.

The battle of Alamein began on October 23rd. 1942.

9. 11. 42.

I expect you have been wondering and very anxious about me this last fortnight. I tried to put as plainly as I could in the last airgraph, that I knew I shouldn't be able to send one for a bit. We actually knew then that we were going into the big bang at the beginning. Since then I have been "otherwise engaged." I am going to get a cable off today somehow to let you know that I am safe and well. We have come out for the time being for a rest. I have hinted several times that we were pretty confident out here, that we could crack Jerry and we've managed to do it - more quickly than any of us dared to hope.

At the moment, no one can say how much longer the campaign will last. That depends on whether he can get enough time to put up another stand. I most sincerely hope that he can't and that we can finish off once and for all the war in N. Africa, which was what we came out to do.

I think you will be relieved to know we all stood up to the "baptism of fire" better than we had expected. It was not as frightening as we had anticipated.

Kenneth Oliver,[*] who is the senior chaplain in our division, came to see us on the morning of the battle. It was grand to see him again. He also left us some "comforts" - a tin of boiled sweets, some strawberry jam, potted paste and so on. That was very welcome in the next few days.

The weather here now is lovely, plenty of sun and just pleasantly warm. We had two nights of sharp showers at the end of last week. The desert looked quite like a picture of the Western Front in the last war, with water standing all over it.

I spent one of those nights in an Italian dug-out, but unfortunately the rain ran in and we were about three inches deep in the morning - fortunes of war. Neither of us seems to have suffered. The sun dried out our stuff quite quickly.

---

[*] Former Toc H staff padre in S.E. London.

12. 11. 42.

I've had a day in Alexandria since I last wrote to you. I thoroughly enjoyed it, and it felt as if I were on leave. Alex is a grand place. The Corniche road along the coast is very fine and the sea, now anyhow, a beautiful blue. There is all the difference in the world between Cairo and Alex. Cairo is definitely oriental, but at Alex, there is a good deal of European influence - French and Greek as well as English. I believe the newspapers are published in English, French, Greek and Arabic. A lot of the best shops are Greek too.

In the afternoon we did a tour organised by the Y.M.C.A. They took us to two pieces of the old Roman Alexandria and then a drive round the city, to the Zoo and along the front. I didn't find the first place - Pompey's Pillar and the site of a temple - terribly interesting. But the second, the Catacombs, was quite different from anything else I had seen. It is morbid, I suppose, to go and see an underground cemetery, but there were carvings of Isis and Osiris and Hoth and other Egyptian Gods, that I had not seen before. The whole place, three storeys high, had been cut out of solid rock and was I suppose, about eighty feet under the surface of the ground.

In the evening we went to the pictures to see Douglas Fairbanks Junior in the "Corsican Brothers". He was the son of his father all right. There was plenty of action and a decent plot and so we enjoyed the film.

I think I told you I had seen recently a play put on by Ensa, "Gaslight". It was by a London company and was really well done. It seemed a little unreal to us to be sitting in a comfortable theatre, watching a first rate play, a couple of days or so after coming down "out of the blue". "In the blue", by the way, is the expression used out here for being in the desert and seeing things.

STAN

I have read the official account of Alamein in the "Battle of Egypt", and I have seen the official diagrams, and have looked at other stories of these eight days too, and yet I have no conception at all of what happened. All I know is that we were told before we went in, that the German army would collapse within ten days and that it collapsed in eight, and of course I know what happened to our crew.

After two days of battle in which we enjoyed ourselves, two nights of travel and a third day during most of which we sat in a narrow lane in a minefield and were shelled almost continuously, we started before first light in a dawn attack. A very few minutes later, our driver called up to the commander, that there was a minefield in front of us. He could see the wire. The commander had no alternative but to order him to reverse. But the wire was on the German side of the minefield; we heard later that Jerry had often "forgotten" to put a wire on our side. As we reversed, we must have run over a mine. None of us heard or felt any particular explosion but this fact was not remarkable, for there was a fair bit of shelling going on all round. Once again the driver called up, this time to say that we had been mined. He could see our left-hand track stretching out on the sand before us and almost immediately the tank stopped.

It was still not light and we sat and waited to see where we were. Soon the outline of a Jerry anti-tank gun showed up some fifty yards or so away from us and we sent a round of H.E. into the pit at the exact moment that another tank of the troop, which had suffered a like fate in the minefield, fired. I saw three of the crew leap out and disappear into what seemed like a communication trench. I could not understand then, and cannot now, why that gun did not fire at us. We were stationary, a sitting prey, and he could have "brewed us up" beautifully.

An hour went by, during which time we kept our eyes tight to the periscopes to watch for other signs of life. Once or twice we saw German infantry and let them have bursts from the Browning. Then the commander asked us if we were willing to have a try at mending the track. Of course, the four of us said "yes", although not very boldly perhaps. The driver and co-driver climbed out of their hatches and the commander and gunner out of the turret. I had just poked my head above when there was an explosion. I looked over the top, and saw only two of the four getting off the sand. The other two were obviously wounded, by what I could not tell then and do not know now.

I had to report these casualties over the air and while I was doing this, the gunner climbed into the turret to say that we were virtually on a machine-gun pit. I pushed my periscope up as much as it would go and squinted out. Sure enough, there was a Browning (!) gun in a sand-bagged pit not five yards in front of our near side wing. Tim, the gunner, and I, decided that now was the time to use the hand grenades which we had carried about with us for so long. And so we lobbed two over the turret. I squinted through the periscope again and saw a timid, frightened, pathetic little German push his face very slowly over the sandbags and then throw his hands up.

Meanwhile the co-driver, Stan, was coping with the two wounded, and coping very well too. Tim went down to bring the Jerry gunner in and I covered him with a Tommy-gun, but was soon called back to the set to give details for the ambulance. Tim came back again with a plan which he had found on the Jerry. It was a careful diagram of distances from his gun; 750 metres to that drum, 300 metres to that hillock and so on. It was while we were examining this plan that I happened to look through the periscope again and could hardly believe what I saw.

Out of the ground were coming forty or fifty Jerries waving white handkerchiefs. For the moment we hardly knew what to do. Once again, though, Tim, with revolver, and I, with "Tommy", went out of the tank to shepherd these prisoners in. But by the time we had jumped down, the prisoners were about 100 in number and as these hundred threaded their way, rather reluctantly, across the minefield, they were joined from all sides by others just as eager to give themselves up. We lined these prisoners up round the tank in order to give our wounded a little cover, and when I finally counted them, there were some 280.

The problem for us now was to know what to do with them. Stan was still tending the wounded. That he made a good job of their wounds was proved by the fact that both had recovered from nasty leg wounds within six months. I was reporting over the air when the M.O. turned up. He looked at our wounded and also the two Jerries who had been brought in in blankets and told us that he would let someone behind know that we had some prisoners to dispose of. Eventually a Bren carrier arrived, and the crew went over the position, now quite clearly a fortified infantry post. They thought everything clear, unfortunately incorrectly, and one of them went with Tim back to the Infantry post with the prisoners. Meanwhile the ambulance arrived and took off our Commander and driver and the two Jerries.

The last we saw of Tim, he was walking lightly alongside the winding column of prisoners. When he came back he must have walked straight into a sniper. He is said to have reeled and fallen. The infantry had been wrong. One man was left and that man got Tim.

A little blue wisp of smoke had excited Stan's curiosity several times and as soon as we knew that a sniper was about, we plastered the spot with H.E. from our big gun. There was no more sniping that day. I am not bloodthirsty at all; in fact, I doubt I am a good fighter. But I hope those rounds of H.E. blew that sniper to hell. He had killed one of our crew.

Then the two of us, Stan and I, settled down to await recovery. The battle was not going well from the wireless accounts. The squadron had gone over the ridge to our left rear and had run on several strongly defended positions. I believe that it had run on as many as six "88's". We reversed our turret in case we should have to fire, and waited. Midday came and went. The afternoon brought almost continuous shelling. From 3 o'clock until 6.30 there was never more than a few seconds between the rounds. And it was during that time that I first got to know Stan well.

I think it must have been to keep both his mind and my own from the full realisation of our position that he talked. He talked for the whole of that $3\frac{1}{2}$ hours, with one break when a tank of the Squadron came to take our ammunition from us. He was a wholesale fruiterer when he joined up, but previously he had done most things. About these jobs, his early life, his wife and daughter, Stan talked for three hours.

During the next eight days I was to know him better still.

That night, just after sunset, our Sergeant-Major came back to the minefield with his own tank, to tow us back. He walked in front of his tank, guiding it away from mines, then hitched a tow-rope on to ours and finally piloted both tanks out. It was a noble piece of work.

He drew us back for some four hundred yards and left us with other tank corpses. We were supposed then to be in safe territory, although the battle was still on the minefield. Naturally, we did not sleep. About 1.50 a.m. a tap came at the tank. Someone was rousing all the crews of these tanks. Jerry had put in a counter-attack and was, according to this fellow, only 150 yards away. We jumped out of the tank and, for the one and only time, left it as it was, kit, equipment, everything intact. We jumped into a truck and were taken about another 400 yards back. Here we found some recovery men who said that they would make an effort to get the tank back.

I remember the Engineers at this point. They were waiting to go into the minefield with their instruments. It was a very cold night and both Stan and I were glad of a cup of their cocoa. After an hour or more our tank was hauled along before us and once again we mounted. It was left this time opposite our regiment - or what was left of it. There were some eighteen tanks only in the leaguer that night; three of the casualties, our own and two others, were there but helpless. And the next morning we saw those eighteen tanks start once more to attempt the job which we had failed in the previous day.

That morning two of the other tanks were taken off to workshop, I presume, and we waited hopefully. The whole day went by, however, and no one came for us. We saw our M.O., who provided us with a hot meal, the first for four days, an N.C.O. of the regiment, who was then travelling with the echelon, and a padre from Brigade. But no recovery section! At last light, everyone moved off and we were left on our own. The battle had swung in our favour and was receding.

Stan and I decided that we must keep guard most conscientiously. Neither liked the idea of being taken unawares. After all, we were still only six to eight hundred yards from the line and we felt that anything might happen to alter the situation. We therefore did two hour turns alternately through the night. When we were "off", we could only sit on the floor of the turret; there was little inclination to sleep.

It was during one of Stan's turns that we thought our fears had materialised. He called me softly and said, "What do you make of this?"

In front of the tank, about a hundred and fifty yards away, was a line of infantry, some 150 or more flat on the ground, and facing our way. It did not make sense. If they were ours, they should surely be facing the enemy. And in any case, why extend in open order there, several hundred yards from where the fighting was? We had seen files wending their way up the track for a couple of hours after last light. On the other hand, if they were not ours, if they were enemy, how had they penetrated to this distance without some sound of battle? Some such reasoning was certainly going through my head and I think, in whispers, we must have argued this with each other. We quite definitely came to the conclusion that the men must be enemy and that before long they would rush the tank.

"What can we do?"

We discussed this problem in whispers too, and decided that if we could turn the turret of the tank to face them, we could dispose of the lot. But we realised that we should never get the turret round. The tank would be rushed first. Then one of the most characteristic traits of Stan's make-up came out. He fears nothing that he understands.

"I'm going to see who they are," he said. He lit a cigarette, quite slowly climbed down from the tank, and walked up to the line. A sergeant raised himself, and in reply to Stan's question, said in broad Scotch,

"We're the Gordon Highlanders and we're waiting for an assignation."

We saw what that assignation was. In a very few minutes six tank transporters drove up and the men mounted. They were off to disputed territory to recover six tanks knocked out in that day's action.

For eight days and nights we waited in that spot and it was not until the fourth there and the ninth in action altogether that we managed to sleep ourselves. On that day several batteries of artillery had brought their 25 pounders up around us and we felt safe. A sergeant of the Sussex Yeomanry came to see us in the afternoon, really, I think, to know if the tank was deserted. He told us that their guns had been moved up for a barrage that night and warned us that his gun, only twenty-five yards in front, would be firing some 400 rounds straight over the tank. We turned in fairly early that night - we needed to after nine days and eight nights without sleep - but it was only the first round of the barrage that I heard. I slept quite soundly through the other 399.

Incidentally, for students of dreams, I had a dream that night, that is worth recording to substantiate the theory that even the most elaborate dreams are stimulated by some outside influence and happen in a split second. I dreamed that a brother of mine had moved his house from London to my home town and settled down in the same road that my parents lived in. He was showing me round the house and finally I noticed that he had the same piano. We began to speak about this piano and he leaned with his elbows on it. In doing so, he kicked the frame and all the strings vibrated - just the noise which a 25 pounder makes when firing.

The artillery was very good to Stan and me. They combed their fellows for any spare cigarettes and even brought us two bottles of beer and some chocolate when their canteen supplies came up. But everyone was very solicitous. A Black Watch officer called in each night to see that we were all right, as did night and morning also, an artillery officer. To him we were a landmark on the famous "Star" track of Alamein. We lacked nothing during those eight days although towards the end our water was getting low. Eventually we were, however, recovered and taken to workshops.

There are many other incidents in this story of our part in the battle of Alamein that I could tell; how we watched "the armour pouring through," as the official version has it, a column of tanks that passed along the next track for nearly twenty-four hours, how on our way back to workshops on November 5th, the front line celebrated Guy Fawkes night with a display of verey lights and tracer, how we eventually "hitch-hiked" back to our regiments, completing the journey on a bren-carrier of the K.R.R.'s with its cheerful cockney crew. But all I will now say is that at the time I was extremely glad that Stan was the fellow to be left with me. He was always cheerful and always hopeful. Sometimes his hope was, to use an outworn phrase, just wishful-thinking, and although I realised then that he was merely expressing his wishful thoughts, I acquired quite an abundance of good humour and hope from them.

H.Q. Squadron. 4th., C.L.Y. M.E.F. 16. 12. 42.

This change of address will probably surprise you. I'm afraid it did me when I heard of it. Unfortunately, the old gang has been split up, and I now find myself alone and with the job of making new friends. At least the name of the regiment means something to me as C.L.Y. stands for County of London Yeomanry. They are a cavalry regiment (now mechanised of course), but we have to give up our berets and wear sidecaps, which I don't want to do.

I was particularly disappointed about the move as negotiations had been going on with the old regiment for lending me for six weeks or so to act as warden for the Talbot House in Alexandria. Only on the morning I knew I was posted, a padre called me over to tell me they had been successful and I should hear something in the course of the day. Actually, the letter about that arrived just two hours too late. You can imagine what not only I, but the Toc H authorities, felt.

There is not much that I can tell you this week. It's been one of saying good-byes chiefly and not therefore very pleasant. It has been cheered up by the news at El Agheila though. I hope this North African affair will be cleared up very quickly now. I don't really mind what happens as long as we get the war finished and get back to a sane life again.

I saw Donald Mathers* round our unit for a day or two before we left. I understand he joined it during the battle, but I only noticed him then. Unfortunately, there never seemed an opportunity to speak to him. He was just going somewhere or we were going and so I left without a word to him. He is really the first chap I've seen that I knew before joining the army and then I didn't have a chat with him. I've had a feeling ever since I've been out here that there must be crowds of people over here that I know and yet I've never bumped into anyone. The world can be a very large place at times as well as a very small one.

---

*Grandson of a neighbour at Bedford.

22. 12. 42.

I am settling down a bit in this mob but I'm still just a little bit "home-sick" for the old unit. The fellows seem very decent. I was talking to one last night who knew Ewhurst well, and the country round about. Actually, he lived at Bookham.

We are in a bit of desert now which is not just all sand. I think the soil must really be quite good as the crops are pushing through quite strongly. There are a number of camels which the Arabs take about grazing just as if they are cattle. There are also herds (or flocks?) of goats. The natives show a little more signs of civilisation - perhaps due to the Italians, as, besides finding their way about on the asses, they also have a few bicycles. Part of their dress here, by the way, is a pair of extraordinary trousers. They have a very low, baggy seat which hangs down somewhere near their knees.

The desert changes from pure sand somewhere about Mersa Matruh. It really is a delight to the eye to see green around one. Halfya Pass (or Hellfire Pass) of course, is rocky. It is quite a big escarpment - a thousand feet or so high, I should guess. The road up it zig-zags like some of the mountain roads in the Alps. At the top though there is just flat desert again, with no corresponding escarpment on the other side. The rocky wall goes right out to the sea and forms a little harbour of Sollum. It looks quite beautiful in the morning light, with the pink reflected on the escarpment.

Tobruk, by the way, is quite small, although large I suppose by comparison with most of these places. Once again the harbour is formed by a promontory sticking some way out to sea.

There are, as you have read in the papers, quite a lot of wrecks in the harbour. There are also caves in the rocks which were used as air-raid shelters, I believe, during the siege of Tobruk. I wish I could describe these places adequately to you and then you would have a picture of what they were like when they are mentioned in the news. I hope they never will be again though, and that their day of interest and importance has gone. It's a bit late to ask now, but I wonder if you have kept these letters. I'm thinking that they would make interesting reading for me when I get back and refresh my memory of lots of little points. I should have liked to keep a diary but we are not allowed to - or at least not allowed to have it with us when we get near action, which makes the whole thing pointless, as it would have to be destroyed with the correspondence.

30. 12. 42.

We had a pretty good Christmas, all things considered. As far as food goes, we probably did much better than you folks at home - turkey and pork, Christmas pudding, oranges and nuts.

There was very nearly a catastrophe as the truck in which the vegetables were being cooked went up in flames.

I've given up really trying to capture any Christmas spirit away from home, though. It is so essentially a home festival, that it is impossible to have a real Christmas away. The few of us, who joined this troop a fortnight ago, managed to be quite merry together, but after all, we are strangers to each other.

I had my bathe in the sea on Christmas day, just to say I had been in the sea on Christmas day, but I hope I'm never again in the climate that will let me repeat this experience.

Last year it was in the frosts and cold winds of Catterick, this year in the desert alongside the Mediterranean. I wonder where next year's Christmas will be spent.

It has been very wet here recently and the desert became a quagmire. We were moving and in some places the roads were well under water. Since then, we have had two or three sunny days and it is drying out quite well.

Our new spot is right on top of a hill, overlooking the sea - quite a beautiful spot in lots of ways. There are some lovely sunsets here. Last night, for example, there was every shade of mauve in the sky and of blue in the sea, with a streak of silver across it. Once again, we are on a rock garden but with patches of grass about.

One disadvantage of the rain and dampness is that it has brought the mosquitoes out. I've never come across a place where there are so many.

There is one fellow who came along here with me whose name is Harry (christened so) Gill. It couldn't be much nearer, could it? He is a very nice chap and has as much character as anyone I've met in the army. I shall probably get to know him better in the days to come.

11. 1. 43.

I haven't yet had any mail since the beginning of December. It seems a long time, but I am consoling myself that when I do get some, it's going to be by the bagful.

As you've gathered from the wireless, we've had a good deal of rain. That apparently is the winter and is likely to last on and off until next month. The "dry water course" as the Ordnance map describes a wadi, does not seem capable of taking the water away. That is the result of being in an undeveloped country. The water stands about until it either disappears into the sand or gets churned into mud by the lorries. There has been a cold wind blowing too. But today the sun is out and it is quite warm in it. The wind, of course, has helped to dry the rain up a bit.

One result of the winter was that I ran a temperature for a couple of days and I have been four days altogether in dock. It was the kind of thing that a warm drink and a night in bed would have cured at home, but here it is hardly possible to give oneself that sort of treatment. Anyhow, it passed off very quickly, and I felt fit again in a very short time.

There really is no news to tell you this week; so I think I had better continue my description of places. I believe the last I got to was Tobruk.

From there onwards the desert gets much more interesting until half way to Bengazi (as the local spelling puts it); it is more like Devon than anywhere else - rolling hills covered with fair sized bushes. Then you get into Musso's colonial belt. Really, it seems tragic that he should have thrown away, by entering the war, all the work that has been done in Libya.

There are small houses, squarish with a balcony, just one storey high with three or four rooms, I should imagine. The ground round about has been cultivated to a greater or lesser extent. Some of the colonists have obviously worked hard. There is wheat showing through and evidences of other crops. All this is left now and I suppose it will go to waste, unless a wandering Arab decides to take a little of it over. There must be hundreds and hundreds of these little farmsteads.

A good number of them are actually on the escarpment, which is over 2,000 feet up in parts. There are two passes to drop down before getting to the lower land around Bengazi. Both of them have hair-pin bends galore. I suppose each drops about a thousand feet and to make it possible for traffic, the road has to zig-zag. This again must have cost Musso a good deal both in money and labour. The view from the top of both is grand. From the first you are looking at the rolling country again to the edge of the escarpment. From the second you are looking over the plain to the sea.

About eighty miles from the second is Bengazi. It looks as if it has been knocked about a good deal - by both sides, I suppose. It is a fair sized city though, much bigger than anything else I've seen out here but Cairo and Alex.

There are queer shallow stretches of water coming right into the land from the sea. The roads are therefore across these flats. The houses are typically Italian and I should imagine there must have been a large number of wealthy Italians in them. Round the town there seem to be some decent boulevards too. The trees are mostly cypress and tamarisk. They are quite large trees here and very delicate.

20. 1. 43.

I hear that there is a whole bundle of mail for me somewhere near the regiment and it is likely to catch up with me in the next day or two.

As you can guess from the news, I've been on the move since I last wrote. Actually, it was an attempt to catch up the regiment after my four days in hospital. Things have moved so quickly that it took me eight days to get back.

We have had some very good news these last few days, haven't we? I expect it has pleased you as much at home as it has us out here.

We know now what it is like to be an "invader". As a matter of fact, it leaves me quite cold. No one seems really to resent our presence and the Arabs of Tripolitania seem really pleased. That is not just wishful thinking but absolutely true.

They are Senussi, and a much cleaner type. Their villages look much cleaner. The huts of stone are not as dilapidated. I think too, that they must be fairly industrious. The wadis are ploughed here and sown. Where we are at the moment, the wadi is full of date palms and is really picturesque. In fact, the desert scenery of the last two days has been some of the very little desert scenery that one could call pleasing. The wadi is charming. It is quite wide, between fairly high hills, some of which rise to cones. There is a green belt at the bottom and on the lower slopes of the hills, there are queer little hummocks where the sand has drifted before the wind against the camel thorn.

In another spot where we bedded down last night, we could see nothing but lilies. They were not particularly beautiful if you looked at them carefully, but in a mass they put a pink shade over the reddish sand and the leaves were a deep green. Right on the ground, without any stalk at all, was another type of lily, more like a small water lily and quite white.

We had an interesting experience yesterday morning. We went into two places, one of Musso's colonial villages, and a town which we had only occupied the day before. The Italians were all hanging about the corners, wondering what was going to happen next, I suppose. There were not many British soldiers in either place and we soon became a centre of attraction. When they found we were only human too, the Ities became quite "friendly". I've put that in inverted commas because they couldn't really welcome us any more than we could really be sorry for them. Anyhow, with the aid of what little Latin we had remembered, we managed to understand some of their Italian and make ourselves understood too. One old fellow spoke French, which eased things a bit.

The colony was once again a fine place which made me feel what a fool Musso had been to risk everything in a war.

There were the bungalows in their plots, again in pairs. A most elaborate system of concrete aqueducts ran from the central well to the fields. The centre of the community was an imposing set of buildings, including a church, a hospital, public dispensary and a colonnade of shops. I didn't see a school, which is a usual part of these colonies. The church was a fine place, with a fresco above the altar, of the colonists offering the produce of the fields. The priest followed us in with what conversation we could manage. I don't know whether he thought we would pillage the church.

I'm wondering what it will be like in Tripoli, because I am convinced it will not be long, a day or two possibly, before we are in there too.

I don't think there has been a terrible lot of fighting in this last phase, nothing like Alamein anyhow. We passed several places where there had been actions, but there was no sign of fighting at all. I hope that means that their army is virtually destroyed.

Continuing our journey westwards - I wonder if it is going to be a circular trip round Africa - we came across today a most interesting Roman, I presume, arena. It was built right on the sea shore. In fact there is only the foreshore between the arena and the sea. It was the typical Roman Amphitheatre, three-quarters of the seating being in very good condition. There were also the foundations of the stage still quite clearly visible.

Nearby was a fort, not nearly as old as many we have come across, or as big. It is quite strange to see one of these Beau Geste fortifications miles away from anywhere. They are larger on the whole than those in the Foreign Legion films, some of them quite formidable. We stumbled on one the other day with a petrol pump in front of it and that was thirty miles or more from the nearest decent road. I think these forts must have been Turkish originally and taken over by the Italians to subdue the Senussi.

As I said before, the folk are very friendly. They come up to us and try to exchange eggs or dates for tea. They have become a tea drinking people for some reason. I expect it is the troops who have made them this, although these here will only have seen Gerries or Ities and I don't suppose they had tea to swap. We haven't had tea to spare and so there is no business with them. Along the roads and the tracks the lads of the village give us a Musso salute. They haven't realised yet that we don't appreciate it and no one has enough Arabic to point the fact out to them.

January 20th. The first troops, 11th Hussars, entered Tripoli.

30. 1. 43.

I still haven't heard from you, or rather, it would be more correct to say, your letters haven't reached me yet. It's almost two months since I heard.

I've just been having a glorious wash-day, beginning with myself and finishing with clothes, towel and so on. It is a lovely day now and things should dry easily in the sun. We have had a fair bit of rain recently though. Wednesday was a terrible day. Even this morning there was quite a sharp frost.

I don't know whether your newspapers have told you. We are now being paid in British Military currency. It consists of notes from 1/- to £1. They are very much the same in quality as the ordinary Treasury note at home. They even have the black thread running through them. The smaller denominations are smaller in size though, even though we've been used to notes of such low value in foreign countries. The official rate of exchange is 480 lira to the pound. I have not been to Tripoli yet though, and so had no chance to spend any of this new currency or receive a handful of small Italian notes in exchange.

I had a chance to go and see the Victory March in Tripoli, after a church parade. The salute was taken by Montgomery. It is the first time I've really seen him, although I've seen his staff car with a glimpse of him inside several times. He reminds me very much of General Harrington who was on the Central Executive of Toc H when I was. In fact, in the distance they might be doubles. There were plenty of news-reel cameras there; so I suppose you will see some of the troops on the screen at home. I'll be there in the crowd watching somewhere but much too obscure to be recognised.

3. 2. 43.

I was hoping to find you something in Tripoli on Sunday which I could send. There was absolutely nothing. The shops all seem to be bazaar like places. The majority of them are closed and those that are open, all seem to be selling the same things; razor blades, any amount of them, soap of a very inferior quality and such like. I suppose there was a good stock of such things for the German and Italian troops.

You say my letter of December 10th. arrived on Christmas Day. I'm afraid that was not a very cheerful one, if my memory serves me correctly. I was feeling a bit "browned off" with things in general. I thought afterwards I shouldn't have let my feelings have penetrated quite so far, but writing home is one of the safety valves.

I hope since that date that they have been more cheerful. They certainly ought to as I have not felt that way since. I have settled down here long since by now. The fellows are a very decent crowd. My job is just the same. This crowd was mechanised at the beginning of the war and although it is called Yeomanry, it is part of the R.A.C. In the old regiment I was on the squadron navigator's tank - I don't think I have told you that before. Here I have been on the Regimental navigator's tank. Unfortunately, we had to leave him at Bengazi, as he had a secondary infection on one finger following a whitlow. I seem to have gravitated towards navigation, but I don't mind. I think it is easily the most interesting part of this kind of job.

I am afraid Philip Parrott's old pupil* was killed at Alamein. He had done very good work that morning, finishing with taking the prisoners we had captured to an infantry post.

Coming back however, he was caught by a sniper. You know I am not bloodthirsty, but the other fellow left on the tank and I had a good deal of satisfaction blasting the sniper to hell.

I did not say anything about Gurney* as we are not allowed to say anything about casualties until they have been announced officially. No one knows what happened to him. His tank and crew just disappeared. Stan Edwards and I were asked a number of times if we had seen anything of them as we were the last to get back to the unit, but we had seen less of them than other people. They just vanished. I

---

*The Tim mentioned in the previous account of Alamein.
*Son of an acquaintance of my mother in Bedford.

heard this week though, that they have now received notification that four of the crew, including Gurney, are prisoners in Italy.

5. 2. 43.

The change of unit took place without as much dislocation as I had anticipated. I knew no one in the batch that came up to the C.L.Y., but I found everyone here quite friendly. I must say that there seems to be two regiments here, the old original Terriers of before the war, and those who have joined since, but I have got to know quite a number, chiefly of the latter kind. I don't suppose I'll make any friendships quite so close as I did with Edwards and Bishop in the old mob. But that was very largely because we had joined the army on the same day at Catterick.

I went to Tripoli on Sunday to see a march-past following a church parade in memory of those who had fallen in the campaign. The salute was taken by Montgomery. I think he must have an eye for the ladies too, as the first thing he did as he arrived at the saluting base was to spot two army nursing sisters. He promptly went across to them and shook hands with them, amid their blushes. Those who marched by were representatives of that part of the Eighth Army that made the last drive.

Tripoli hasn't quite made up its mind where it stands, I think. The shops are more like the bazaars in the native parts of Cairo, very small indeed, even in the main roads. This seems all wrong as the buildings themselves are quite imposing, with the usual colonnades as shade from the heat of the sun. But under these colonnades are only these poky shops.

One difficulty at the moment is that there is nowhere for a soldier to get any food. Quite rightly, the local population has been forbidden to serve meals to troops, so that the Goebbels can't say that the British troops are eating their food.

All that can be bought is a cake. As the Arab, who sells it, only knows one English coin yet, the shilling, one has to pay a shilling for a smallish slab of this cake. Everything is a shilling.

They don't yet seem able to cope with any more of our monetary system. Incidentally, we are now paid in British Military Currency, which is pounds, shillings and pence, and have now done with piastres, at least for the time being - and I hope forever.

Tripoli itself must have been a lovely place under normal conditions. The promenade along the front is really between two moles which form the harbour. The western one is the famous Spanish mole which you have heard so much about in Air Force communiqués. There isn't a lot of this left now. Almost in the centre of the promenade is the castle, an old Turkish fort, I should think. In its way it is quite beautiful and romantic looking. It has a Union Jack flying from it, for the first time in its history, I understand. Next are two columns with Romulus and Remus on the top of one, and a Roman galleon on the other. From there the main roads of the town radiate. On the fort is a plaque commemorating the "Redemption" of Libya in 1912, and Mussolini has sacrificed all this for his insane ambitions.

I wonder what the reaction to the fall of Tripoli has been at home and how the press have built it up. I myself felt certain it would happen since long before Alamein and as the objective was approached bit by bit, I'm afraid I lost consequently any real sense of excitement. I can imagine you at home going from place to place on a map as the daily advances were announced.

It is difficult for you at home to imagine distances out here, isn't it? Churchill, in a speech which I did not hear, made the point that the advance of the Eighth Army from Alamein to Tripoli was as far as London to Moscow. And this had been done in eighty days, at the rate of eighteen miles a day. I believe it has taken me fifteen days of travel to get from Alexandria and on some days we did as much as one hundred and eighty miles. A run of twenty five miles or even fifty means nothing at all. The fifteen days, of course, have been spread out since I left the last unit.

18. 2. 43.

Your Christmas telegram came this week. It doesn't matter a bit that it was six weeks late. The wishes mean just as much to me. I hope my letters are getting through and that you have had most of mine by now.

This delay is inevitable really though, and is a healthy sign. The further west we go - and the nearer home we get, the more difficult it is to get the mail to us. Almost certainly, the route the letters have to take after they have finished their air journey, is more troublesome and devious. By the way, what I have just said reminds me of a quotation Winston used to some troops out here - not us, he didn't speak to us.

"You nightly pitch your moving tents a day's march nearer home."

The news is quite good now, isn't it? I've just been reading an Egyptian Mail of February 14th. I've not seen one so recent for a long time. Russia seems to be rolling the Gerries back properly. I hope we can keep the initiative now. We must if we possibly can, and at the moment it looks difficult for Hitler to find anywhere where he can really open up an offensive. I hope the Yanks and the 1st Army manage to contain him until the 8th Army can join up with them. If they do, then this year may bring us very appreciably nearer the end.

Evie talks of the excitement of buying new cups and saucepans and kettles. I suppose everything must be getting very short. If you can't get an iron kettle, you'll have to do what we do for a brew pot. We keep a big tin that has had seven lbs. of jam or margarine in it, put a wire handle on and then when it gets too dirty on the outside or too tanned on the inside, it can be thrown away and another used. We have not done badly for food at all. Our main stay is M and V or meat and vegetable ration. We can stew this or fry it or use it with a tin of bully and some bashed biscuits in rissoles. It makes them very tasty. We have had some oatmeal recently for porridge. I rather fancy this was left behind by the Italians. The biscuits are not the great big dog biscuits of the last war. In size they are about as big as an ordinary biscuit. They are pretty hard but they can be soaked and fried in bacon fat, soaked and mashed as an alternative when the oatmeal has run out, or powdered and used almost as flour. I think we must be very much better fed than the soldiers of the last war, from the stories of the old sweats of that time.

We forget most times that we are fast becoming the old sweats of this war. As they learnt to conquer the mud, we have learnt to conquer the desert. Here it is not so much a stationary game as getting into the habit of packing up quickly for a move and getting oneself organised quickly at a stop.

25. 2. 43.

I hope my letters are getting through to you better now. I sent off to Evie sometime during the week a letter with a copy of the Tripoli Times in it. I thought it might interest you all. The authority started producing these news sheets about a week after Tripoli was occupied. They have the English news printed on one side and Italian news on the other. The wog newspaper boys are selling them for two cigarettes instead of two lira. I think there must be a shortage of tobacco in Tripoli.

The city has become much more normal than when I last mentioned it. Far more shops are open, but they all seem to be very small, tiny, insignificant boxes. There is very little in them, although I did manage to get a good pair of braces for 2/6. I think I paid 4/6 for the last pair I bought at home. It is really a pleasant place though. I wish I had seen it in peacetime conditions.

I have been to a Toc H meeting there. There were about fourteen there - most of them not members of Toc H but contacts through the Forces. I imagine it will be difficult to keep a unit running as people are not stable enough. If there are only one or two to keep the thing going, it is worth while though, for casuals like myself. There was no one that I actually knew there. The Y.M.C.A. has opened a club now and it is interesting to go in and see what a large Italian house is like. The rooms are rather ornate, with marvellous wrought-iron candelabra, for example. There were marble floors with a pattern in them, and no fireplaces. The furniture has been taken over with the building, I should think, as it was Italianate again. Even the Itie wireless sets had been left and we managed to get the news on them. I was glad as I hadn't heard the English news for some time.

The weather, by the way, is grand now. The sun seems to have its summer brilliance again, and the Med. is the real Mediterranean blue again. I can see it two or three hundred yards away as I write. I haven't been in it yet - I don't know how warm it is.

8. 3. 43.

My record mail was awaiting me last night - twenty-nine letters and what not. Your letters of Nov. 25th, Dec. 2nd, 20th, 28th, letter cards of Jan. 15th, 23rd, and 30th and airgraphs of Jan. 27th, Feb. 5th, and 11th, were among them. I saw the other day a list of what has happened to mail both ways. It seems to be making the main part of its journey very quickly, in anything between five and fourteen days, but some of it is definitely lost - both ways.

I started to read this packet when I got it at about 4 o'clock and hadn't finished by the time it was dark. The remainder helped to pass the time, two hours, of wireless watch, in the middle of the night, very pleasantly and as a matter of fact, I read all yours again during that two hours too. The watch is pretty boring usually, as there is little or nothing to do, but sit with headphones on in case of necessity. Needless to say, I was very glad to get all the news. I hope by this time my letter cards have started to come in again. If you keep a watch on the communiqués, you will get a rough idea of when my letters are likely to be delayed. It is not so much that I can't write, as that when things are on the move, it is very difficult for the authorities to get the mail back to make the long journey.

I'm hoping that you will hear some good news of this magnificent(!) Eighth Army before this letter reaches you. There is a terrific spirit of confidence here at the moment, and as important I think, every man realises that Montgomery is a wizard.

By the way, according to Churchill, when our children ask us what we did in the war, it will be enough to say, "I marched with the Eighth Army." I often wish I was away from here if only to see the whole of this North African campaign from a more detached angle. I think you at home probably feel the excitement of great events more than we do here. I hope by the time you read this, more great events will have happened, and that Rommel will be out of Africa. He certainly has been no match for Monty yet. By the way, just before we put M and V (meat and vegetable ration) in the frying pan, he went by on the track near us. No salutes or anything like that, but a wave from the fellows as they looked round and saw who it was, and a friendly wave back from Monty.

The spring flowers are fully out now. This morning in the first light before dawn, the ground was covered with a spread of the most delicate blue. You know how we used to admire the blue of the lupins in the twilight - we were never up to appreciate it at 5.45. It turned out to be stock, which smelt beautifully last night. There are three kinds here, blue, white and yellow, very much like night-scented stock. There is a whole host of other flowers quite common to England too - no end of yellow daisies, scabius, periwinkle and poppies. The most common of these is a dark magenta in colour and about the size of Iceland poppies. I have come across one or two really royal purple ones too.

You asked about Eighth Army slang. One finds oneself using quite a number of Arabic words: "Maleesh" is the present equivalent of "San fairy ann" or "Ça ne fait rien" or "It doesn't matter". "Sayeeda, George" is a common greeting. "Sayeeda" means Hullo, and George is the word every Tommy was called in Egypt. "Mafeesh" is finished, "chai" tea, "felous" money and so on and so on. Yes, there is quite a lot of slang from the Arabic.

I had a great thrill out of the view last night. You will have read of the mountains that run in a semi-circle - or rather, more from Homs to somewhere on the Tunisian coast - I don't know the exact point - yet. Just at sunset the particular part we could see looked marvellous. In the sky and the mountains there was every pastel shade of red and blue and combination of the two colours that you could imagine, and the outline of the mountains was just a sharp silhouette. I wish I could describe it more adequately. I like to feel that you are all sharing my experiences.

10. 3. 43.

I was very glad to hear about Albert Gurney. As I have already told you, I knew he was a prisoner, but not that he had been wounded too. This I have passed on to his old unit via Harold Collins. As I explained, we are not allowed to say anything about casualties until they have been officially announced, and although I felt there was a strong possibility that he was a prisoner, I could have given Mrs. G. no comfort from any knowledge that I had. Hence it was much better for you to know nothing. As a matter of fact, the sergeant-major and others thought that the tank must have been hit and burnt out as there was no trace of it. I was the only one who felt the crew might have become prisoners. I could see quite well how that could have happened from my own experience.

You mentioned in one letter about my companions. I'm afraid we are all scattered now. I knew no one at all of the very few who came to this unit. Bishop is away in one direction; Stan Edwards after his spell in hospital, is in a workshop job in Alex. Hal Collins is with the old mob. They are now on a totally different job and very much reduced in numbers; that is the reason why over half of us had to go.

The fellows in this mob are a very decent crowd. I've made a number of good pals already. Although originally the fellows were Terriers from London, they come from all over the place now. The crew I am on now has one from Doncaster, one from Carlisle, and one from Glasgow - all Northerners, you see.

It is a pity that the other crew broke up, but that was inevitable when the officer left us, and then I went into hospital and both on the same day. The officer, by the way, was a Gladstone of the G.O.M. family. He is a cousin of the present Lord Gladstone, and his estate manager or something of the sort. He is an Old Etonian with bags of money. I'm sorry we have lost him, if only for the time being, as I was getting on very well with him. The regiment had quite a number of notables in it. The present second-in-command is Lord Cranley, (another way of spelling Cranleigh), the heir of the Earl of Onslow, whose family house is at Guildford.

I heard from the driver of our tank at Alamein. He is now at Pietermaritzburg and making a very good recovery. He can walk without a stick and with only a slight limp. I am most surprised as I felt sure the tendons behind the knee were severed. Anyhow, he hopes soon to be on the way back North. The tank commander has already left for the North. I thought both these had finished with the war.

About listening to the news. I believe the time I mentioned it we were moving up to Alamein on the first night. We heard it as we were moving along on our own tank wireless - shortwave of course. We listened the next two nights too. We were very anxious to hear what the B.B.C. was saying of us. On that occasion too we wanted to know how soon you would be told that a full-scale offensive had been opened. Now we hear the news on the one or two sets that there are about the regiment - I have heard it this afternoon. We are just as anxious to know what the opinion is of Rommel's latest little mistake in coming out of the Mareth line and getting so pounded. We can't possibly get a true picture of what is happening. More often than not, we have no idea of what is going on. Although I must say this, that everyone of us is given as complete a picture of what the plan is, as is humanly possible. I was amazed before Alamein at how many details of the plan we were told and that, four days before the offensive opened.

I am very sorry it was impossible to buy anything worthwhile in Tripoli. And I don't suppose it will be any better in Tunis or Bizerta or wherever is our next big city.

Actually, I believe the Gerries had systematically cleared Tripoli of everything - or the Italians. I am equally convinced that a lot of the shops had not been opened for a long time. Part of the "Tripoli back to normal" plan seemed to include the making of shelves and showcases for the shops. There are far more opened now, but they still have little or nothing in them.

I believe the population is not well fed. Once again probably, the food was taken before we entered the place. Quite small children used to come up to us - Italian as well as Arab - and ask for a biscuit. I saw Arabs going along the gutter, picking up monkey nuts which had fallen. Of course I don't know how much of this is due to circumstances and how much is habit. The Arabs don't seem to mind our occupation at all. A lot of them are employed by the British now, road making, at petrol dumps and jobs of that description. I suppose we can afford to give them a decent wage compared to what they have been used to.

It is getting quite warm in the sun these last few days, although the weather has been changeable. Two days ago we were saying it was warm enough for K.D. shorts and shirts again, but there is now a wind and we have certainly wanted our battle dress.

It is very much more pleasant to see some green around now. Churchill assured us that we should see much more palatable scenery for the rest of the journey, but unfortunately, as soon as we left Tripoli, we saw little but sand. The native houses hereabouts are some of the worst I've seen. They just consist of mats made of grasses and put round poles. The roofing is just a mass of these mats slung over at any angle. I suppose the diameter of the whole thing would not be more than eight to ten feet across, and the whole family appears to do everything inside. There are some stone buildings about. They are rather like air-raid shelters, a rectangle of stone, say 10ft. by 6ft., with a semi-circular roof. The camel is still the ship of the desert. They are the beasts of burden all right, and do the ploughing or anything else that seems necessary. The ass is the bicycle, and there are just a few beautiful Arab horses. One gentleman we saw had a magnificent saddle cloth and stirrups more like steps in size - a plate the whole length of his foot with a triangular piece, beaten with a design, coming up to the leather strap.

I've started making a list of all the people you mention that have wished to be remembered to me. Thank them all very much and give them my best wishes. A special congratulation to Miss Geary on her 82nd. birthday.

March 13th. to 20th. The assault on the Mareth Line.

12. 3. 43.

You say people at home are cautious - or were at the beginning of December - about events out here. They have every right to be and the last thing that is going to help is easy optimism. The fellows here are just the same. At the moment we are all wondering how hard the Mareth line is going to be to crack, whether it will be as difficult as Alamein, for example. I myself believe that once the job begins, we shall find Gerry prepared for rear guard actions to protect the evacuation. Then it will be the turn of the Navy and the Air Force to prevent a Dunkirk. We have been told that the view of last Saturday's dust-up, when Rommel sent forty tanks out from the Mareth line and lost thirty, without our losing one, is that the whole affair was very amateurish. However, we have already achieved enough to give folks at home some confidence in British weapons (and Yank) and the fighting qualities of the British soldier. That is not mere jingoism.

I can't say that any of the crew I was with at the time, worked themselves up before they went into battle. As a matter of fact, we were extremely phlegmatic. We lazed about in the sun all the day, Oct. 23rd. - had a good wash, changed our clothes, tidied up the tank a bit and so on. We did a 28 mile approach march that evening, during which time we read "Punch" and "Time", an American magazine, listened to the news at eight o'clock, (6 o'clock then by your time), and were generally amazingly calm. Incidentally, we took the 250 prisoners in about ten minutes. They just appeared from the ground with white handkerchiefs and threaded their way through the minefield towards us. It was just as if the ground had opened up and these fellows came out of boxes. We didn't know that we had been mined on an infantry position. But all that seems a very long time ago - it's four months exactly. I wonder what the next four months will bring.

I don't know that the water in the radiator presents much difficulty. I have never been on a truck that has boiled, and our tank at Alamein maintained a steady engine temperature of 160 degrees. All trucks carry sand channels, perforated steel plates about 4ft. long which are used only as a last resort if the truck is ditched. We usually dig out, that is, dig a channel, an inclined plane for the truck to run up. There is not much bogging though really. Most of the trucks have four-wheel drives and can get across quite soft sand. They are supposed to be more efficient generally than the Gerries' tracked transports, which are necessarily slower.

Of course, navigation has a lot to do with this. The navigator must pick a course on the map which looks passable and even then must make detours if he comes to any really soft stuff. We in the old mob used a sun compass, a very simple but most efficient instrument. It does away with all the problems a magnetic compass presents. We had a magnetic compass on the tank but it was U.S. in both senses of the term - Yankee and also unserviceable. We took the tank out to try the compass one day. It read quite differently - as much as fifteen degrees in some parts on two rounds of the circuit. Then we found it jumped on or back several degrees, every time the driver changed gear, and on one occasion we proved that it changed its reading when the tools in the tool box were placed back differently. Hence our preference for the sun compass. The method usually used with a magnetic compass is to use a hand one outside the tank - 30 or 40 yards away - line the tank on its bearing, then for the driver to pick an object straight ahead and drive on it. The bearing must be checked every quarter of an hour or so. That makes the method slow, and also, in the really sandy parts of the desert, there are no landmarks to drive on, not even a bush or a bit of scrub.

You will keep "The Battle of Egypt", won't you? I want to see and read it very much. I have very little idea of how the battle was won. It seems a miracle to me. We were told, before we went in, that Gerry would crack within ten days. On the seventh it still didn't seem possible to us, where we were, but on the eighth it had happened. Of course, it is impossible to get anything like a complete view of operations.

The pipers in Tripoli remind me very much of Goldington Road[*] in the last war. You remember the nightly to-do there.

The bands did this in Tripoli in the square before the castle. I think we were out to impress the local population. Certainly, the bands were extremely smart. The guard changing which took place too, was just as impressive as outside Buckingham Palace. I wonder

---

[*]At Bedford.

what the local population, particularly the Arabs, thought of the pipes. They all looked most curiously at the whole affair.

14. 3. 43.

I really do hope some of my mail has got through to you by this time. I can't understand what has happened to it. No, I very rarely hear a B.B.C. programme in the desert. If it is at all possible, we like to gather round to hear the news, but we don't manage this very often. There are not really many civilian sets about now, but we all flock anxiously to them if we hear the signature tune of the news. They use "Hearts of Oak" for that, by the way. We realise the news is several days old, but it is the only way we have of getting a general picture of what is happening. Sometimes we know far more details than the B.B.C. give - for example, Rommel's little adventure last weekend. We hear a large number of rumours though, and the wireless helps us check up on them.

I've said "in the desert" but that is becoming more and more just a habit. Although the ground is basically sand now, it is more and more cultivated. For part of the time this week we were in corn and it only needed to ripen too. Just fancy, full ears in March! There are far more wells too. I suppose one could find a well every mile or so, if one was to look. Some are very deep and we have no rope that will reach the bottom.

Some are only just under the surface though, and we can reach the water with our arms. That will tell you that the country is fairly hilly. It is certainly much more interesting than the flat Libyan plains.

22. 3. 43.

Last night I managed to hear Churchill's speech. A little group of fellows, twelve or fifteen, gathered round a truck in a wadi to listen. I was extremely pleased I heard it as I thought it was one of his best. I know our main job is to win the war, but I believe it is going to be very much harder to win the peace, and if a good deal of thought isn't put into this now, when we get back to a more normal state of things, we shall just find the most comfortable armchair, a pair of slippers and a pipe and relax. From what we've been able to read of Churchill's previous speeches, he hasn't been particularly willing to commit himself about post-war problems, but last night he certainly did. That is what pleased me. A lot of chaps seemed disappointed, and wanted to hear about the marvellous Eighth Army and its exploits, but I feel the less said about victory until we actually have it, the better, and the more said and pledged about what is to happen afterwards, the better again.

I had to put this down in the middle of that little sermon, as a minor catastrophe happened. There was a terrific storm, including hail. After a short while it started finding its way into the bivvy and we had to rush about madly doing things. Fortunately we got to it in time, but there are a number of fellows flooded out. Some of their bivvy holes look like slipper baths. Just in front is a wadi. There was a real torrent for half an hour or so. We've had two or three more showers since, but none as bad as the first and so perhaps now I can get on with the letter. The weather is most changeable though. In spite of the hail, it is quite muggy. The other night we had thunder and in between there have been really cold March winds.

82

4. 4. 43.

*We had a little incident yesterday that broke the normal run of things. One of our tank crew had been on guard the night before and was missing at reveille. It was quite obvious that he had wandered in the dark - it was black and the stars were hidden by clouds - and got himself lost. The only thing to do is to sit down and wait until it is light. The amusing part of the story was the description sent out by the second-in-command over the wireless.

"Lost, a strange little man answering to the name of Davies, usually wears a scarf on his head and P.T. shoes without laces, walks with his head forward and has a habit of shouting at you."

He turned up about an hour after it was light. He had wandered three or four miles away.

---

*I have left this letter in, although a much fuller account of the incident comes in the following pages.

DAVE

Dave was a Northerner, a sort of a music hall turn. He was, as he called himself, really wicked, and yet he had a good heart and was good company. He had a number of stock phrases which he would produce at all odd times.

"May I borrow (in a perfect Oxford accent) your me-ap case, George?" "Oh yes, please de-oo." He had his stock recitations, "Gunga Din" and "Dangerous Dan Magrew," and these he produced on average every other day. He was the clown of the tank crew for several months.

Dave was no good at cooking. He used to look after the fires and always made the brew of tea. I believe he had a reason for doing this job; he liked to lick the milk spoon. It was a great help to the cooks, however, if someone would see to the fires. An empty petrol tin, with the necessary holes cut in it, gets a dirty object when used as a fire and carried on the back of a tank, and the cook's hands would pick up soot and dust if he had to touch it.

We always looked after ourselves, of course. We would carry quite a quantity of rations, sometimes as much as ten or twelve days' supplies, when we were not anticipating visits from the Quartermaster for some time. Then we had our petrol tin fireplace, a tank cooker, usually not very satisfactory, especially if made in Cairo, a frying pan and various pots, most important of which was the brew-pot. All these pots originated from the same source - seven pound potato tins. We became most inventive in our use of tins; there were half a dozen designs for fires alone, with Marks I, II, III, etc., and two or three for brew-pots. We became as inventive in our cooking too.

The main constituents of the rations were naturally bully beef and biscuits, with M. and V. (Meat and Vegetable) a very close third. We learnt half a dozen or so ways to serve bully, from just plain cold - in my opinion the best way - to rissoles. These would contain quite a proportion of "bashed" biscuits and onions, if we could get any. "Bashed" biscuits were most useful. We used the haft of the pick from the tank to grind the biscuits into as small particles as we could. They were the main ingredient of "biscuit burgoes" which was a breakfast standby throughout the campaign. We always liked porridge for breakfast, however hot it was, and when the oatmeal had run out, we made it of these bashed biscuits. "Crusader", the Eighth Army Weekly, gave an explanation of the word "burgo" as Scotch for porridge, and introduced among the Turks by Scottish soldiers at the time of the Crimean War, brought by the Turks to Egypt and picked up again by the soldiers of this war. Whether that explanation is right or not, "burgoes" meant biscuit porridge. The biscuit crumbs were soaked, boiled and served with as much milk and sugar as circumstances would allow.

At one time we had a craze for making biscuit cakes. We built ovens of petrol or ammunition tins, with a round container as a chimney. The chimney invariably caught fire. The recipe for the biscuit cakes would read in "Mrs. Beaton" as follows:-

"Bash two packets of biscuits, add two dessert spoonfuls of flour, if any, and as much margarine, if any. Rub the margarine in. Add sugar, if any, to taste, and raisins, chopped prunes, chopped monkey-nuts, lemon-juice and rind, or anything that will give the cake a taste. Mix with water into a fairly stiff paste. Cook in the oven until smoke comes from the door." These cakes were really palatable and a very good way of eating army biscuits.

As we travelled further along the North African coast, it was possible to supplement our rations by bartering. The wogs seemed to want tea above all things. When they acquired the tea-drinking habit, no one could tell me. It could not have been a native taste and yet I should not have thought that they would have acquired it from either German or Italian soldiers, both from non-tea drinking countries. But "chai" it was they demanded, and very seldom received.

At one time we had a number of eggs. For five, on one occasion, we let a little tea go, just a mere pinch; but I think that was the only time we could spare any. On another occasion we had looked out an old pair of civvy shoes, on which we set the price of eighteen eggs. During the morning along came the inevitable band of wogs. We showed them the shoes and indicated eighteen on our fingers. They shrugged their shoulders and said "ten". We turned back to the tank and they raised their offer to twelve. They gave us to understand that they had no more and so we looked into their basket. There surely were eighteen eggs and fine ones too. We said "Cooloo", our Arabic coming into service, but they still persisted in twelve, and so we climbed back into the tank and continued with our work, while the wogs slowly made off. Some thirty yards away they stopped and went into a huddle. Back they came and offering the basket, said "Cooloo". We said "Aiwa" or "yes", and jumped down. Then fortunately, the rogue in Dave came out. He took the basket, saying "Shufti." He counted the eggs but there were only fifteen. The Arab said that there were only that number before, but Dave gave him a fair piece of his mind. The Arab couldn't have known what the words meant, but he must have picked up the meaning from the tone. He looked like a schoolboy just discovered in some misdemeanour and very sheepishly dived into his blanket to produce two eggs. By our computation, two and fifteen didn't make eighteen, and so Dave began again. If the previous effort had produced two eggs, this second should have produced a dozen. While it was proceeding, the victim shook his head, assuring us he had no more, until finally he had had enough, wilted, and found the eighteenth egg from somewhere in his voluminous folds.

Another time one of our officers went round buying sheep, of the real Berber type, which, incidentally, were mostly black with long ears. Two butchers in the regiment got to work and we had several meals (for which we paid) of lamb, and very good it was too. We had a tin of peas in our rations at that time and enjoyed lamb chops and peas.

We were by this time in a much more cultivated part of the North Africa coast. There is a coastal area round Bengazi, which stretches for some hundred miles eastwards, I suppose, and forty or fifty miles southwards and in which it is possible to see Mussolini's African Empire. From the top of Tocra Pass, which leads down from the desert escarpment to the coastal plain, the countryside is dotted with the little white bungalows of the colonists. There is another area round Misurata and again round Tripoli. But all the settlements seem to be smallholdings, and worked by the Italians themselves. They centre on community buildings, a church, shops, hospital, schools, dispensary and clinic. I went into one of these centres on the morning on which it had fallen into our hands. The Italian population was gathered in little groups on the corners, obviously wondering what was going to happen to them. But the sheet hanging from the flag pole of the hospital had been enough; the war had passed them by. The priest wandered into his little church after us, expecting us to do some damage, I expect, if the German propaganda had penetrated at all. He was very pleased, however, to stand and talk to us, as best he could, about his church and little flock. I must say again that this community was entirely Italian; their colonial policy seems to have done nothing for the native Arab.

In Tunisia, on the other hand, the Arab seemed more prosperous. His houses were of stone in the main, not the filthy, squalid round tents of Tripolitania, although they were really just as filthy. These stone houses had round roofs and were rather like surface air-raid shelters. His flocks were larger in number and he had horses, which one seldom sees earlier. I remember on one occasion a frantic Arab rushing about our tents trying to unhobble some twenty horses, while, and because, I suppose, the shells were falling around. He himself did not look as clean as his brother in Libya. For one thing, the Semussi there wears a white blanket which is almost invariably awry, while the Berber of Tunisia wears a brown blanket, unfortunately usually filthy.

There seem to be no smallholdings in Tunisia either. Around Sfax and Susse there is little else but the olive groves, miles and miles of them with their trees planted in the straightest lines imaginable. Higher up near Tunis, there are the Wheatlands, and on both, Arab labour is employed. It seemed all wrong to see a wog in his native dico driving a tractor.

We were by this time well past that strange frontier just between Tripolitania and Tunisia. We saw with a fair amount of satisfaction the tricolour flying again over the Customs House on the Tunisian side. When we first passed this station, the enemy was round about Ben Gardane; in fact we moved up because a report had come in that forty German tanks had ventured out from that village. We saw nothing of them, however, as they then returned to the Mareth line proper. We did very little before Mareth, though, apart from some infantry support work. We were for some time in the shell range, and when Gerry decided to send some rounds over, we had a steeplechase to see who could get into the tank first. After all, a tank is a first class splinter-proof shelter.

Usually Dave would win.

When we came back, we could see how strong the Mareth defences were and marvelled at the Guards getting as far as they did before they were driven back. Out there we were not alarmed, as Mr.

Churchill seemed to be, when he announced in the Commons that we were almost back to our starting point. We knew that the New Zealanders and others had gone round on the "left hook" and that soon the Mareth positions would be untenable. Incidentally, Mr. Churchill must also have known this. We were ready on March 6th. to tackle Rommel's Panzers when he made his little trip towards Medenine, and there was no need for us to go into action. The anti-tank guns knocked out some fifty tanks that day. A fortnight later, we went across the battlefield and it looked from the "corpses" of the Gerry tanks as if they had panicked. They were standing facing all directions and some had obviously reversed into others or caught wings and had become entangled. It was pretty easy to imagine a very thorough "flap" when our anti-tank guns opened up at very short range. When we eventually moved through the Mareth line, we passed through seven continuous miles of minefields, such were the defences.

The next point to be tackled was at the Wadi Akarit and our success there seemed to us individual soldiers the most decisive in the North African campaign. If he could have held us there, the enemy would have prevented the Eighth and First Armies linking and might have defended the Tunisian corner indefinitely. But it was the last naturally defensive position before the hills around Tunis and, I say again, it appeared to the common soldier that his inability to hold at Akarit decided the issue in North Africa.

The fighting that day was as bloody as anywhere in the campaign. He must have been taken by surprise, but a surprised rat will fight. Two or three hours after the infantry had gone in, I was talking to a corporal who had just come back from the wadi itself, and he said he had seen a mobile brothel put out by our barrage and the bodies of women from it, in the front line. When we eventually went through the line, we also saw the van of one of these brothels ditched by the side of the road.

This ride through was one of the most nightmarish experiences. We made it after dark on a pitch black night. The path, cut through the mines, was only just wide enough to take our tank and there were some very awkward corners. The corners were marked by pin-point lights, with hurricane lamps under petrol tins. The tapes along the path were almost impossible to see in the dark. Our driver crept along with the tank commander and myself watching from the turret and ready to shout into the microphone if the occasion arose. At some corners it was necessary to reverse in order to turn and we watched the rear of the track with great anxiety. To warn us, along the track, were tanks, trucks and even an ambulance that had come to grief. I suppose it took us no more than ten minutes to make the passage, but it seemed more like two hours to us.

It was somewhere during the Mareth-Akarit stage of the campaign, that the funniest incident of all happened to Dave. Normally we went into "close leaguer" at night. I have often wondered what is the derivation of the word "leaguer"; I see from the dictionary that it means "the camp of a besieging or beleaguering army," and comes from the Dutch word, "laager".

We used the term, as I suppose it was used in the South African war, to mean to settle down together without actually pitching a camp; and therefore does it not have some cognition with "league," or "combine together"? In a close leaguer the three battle squadrons would take up position in front and on the flanks, the R.H.Q. vehicles would come inside in two lines with about a ten to fifteen yard interval, and the forward echelon would once again come inside these two lines. The regimental "family" would then at night cover a very small area; I often thought at night how much like a family it was, how self-contained and complete, for the moment.

During the Mareth-Akarit times we more often stayed on open leaguer or closed in only a little, and to not nearly so close an interval. Such positions made it very much more difficult for the guard; it could not go from vehicle to vehicle as in a close leaguer; it had to rely on remembering what features there were in the leaguer, and this feat of memory was not easy, as frequently we had only seen the site for a few minutes in daylight before leaguering. On one such occasion, Dave was on guard in a middle turn somewhere about two o'clock in the morning. At half-past five, when we should have been up and on the air, we were just waking up the remainder of the guard, in a "flap". They had not woken up and consequently had not called reveille for the squadron. The other sentries realised that Dave had not called the next turn and his bed was empty. They began searching for him round about but without success. Then the second-in-command got on the air. "A.B.C., A.B.C." (or whatever the call sign that day was).

"Lost or strayed a funny little man, probably wearing a sock on his head and P.T. shoes, wears glasses, walks with a forward stoop and is inclined to shout at you when he speaks. This man is dangerous, return him to us." We had our breakfast and still there was no sign of Dave. Then about half-past seven he wandered in. He had walked on and on until suddenly he realised that he was lost.

He had made several attempts to get back, but there were no stars to use and he found himself thoroughly confused. He therefore decided to wait until he heard the tanks start up at first light and to walk towards the sound. When it was light, he found himself beyond the forward infantry. It had taken him more than an hour to walk back from where he had heard the first tanks. We had heard frequently of fellows who were lost in the desert on guard, but the first in our squadron would be Dave. I shall always now think of him as the "funny little man wearing a sock on his head".

April 1st./2nd. The Battle of Akarit.

12. 4. 43.

I hope by now you will have got my telegram for next Friday. It will let you know that I was all right after the Mareth affair and I hope this gets to you quickly, to let you know that I am safe and sound after Akarit, and up to date. But remember what I have told you over and over again. "No news is good news."

I am writing this among the olive groves. I don't know whether your newspapers have stressed that it really is olive country that the Eighth Army has passed through recently. I heard one mention of it on the wireless the other night when it was announced that Sfax had fallen. There seem to be miles and miles of these groves. The trees look old and very well established and in a perfect geometric pattern too, all straight lines. Actually this part of Tunisia shows signs of much longer colonisation than Tripolitania, or more precisely, Cyrenaica.

The olive seems to be an evergreen and has quite a narrow leaf, dark green on one side and very light on the other, so that they appear almost grey.

We came through a town the other day, which for a moment had better remain nameless, and got a terrific welcome from the French population. It looked to me as if it was genuine, too. The townsfolk were crowding the road along which we passed - it had only been occupied a few hours earlier. They clapped and cheered and gave the V sign. I felt the Victory V really meant something to them. From somewhere or other a number of Tricolours and even Union Jacks and Stars and Stripes had been produced in such a short time, and red, white and blue favours were being worn. I suppose it means a lot to see British Troops marching (or rather riding) through after an occupation by the Germans. We did a real Churchill drive through the adoring mob, bowing and waving from side to side - and I must admit that a lump came into my throat more than once.

I hope that we have got to the last stage of this African campaign. I wonder if Rommel can put up a stand anywhere now - you will know the answer to that before you get this letter. We really seem to have caught him on the wrong foot at Akarit. I heard from a fellow that he was so unprepared for the attack that he had his mobile brothels almost in the front line. This fellow had himself seen the women from it killed by our barrage. It was a grand breakthrough and I hope it will prove decisive.

No, I haven't the slightest idea what a cactus lupin is like. But it reminds me that there are a fair number of cacti round here. The native compounds (is that the right word?) seem to have low earth walls built round them and growing on the top are large flat cacti. They are prickly and seem to grow anywhere or nowhere.

We did a bit of bartering the other day. We got two eggs for a packet of cigarettes and made an omelette of them. This was so good, in fact the best omelette I've ever made, I think, that it tempted us to swap a pinch of tea, ever so little, believe me, for five eggs, which the four of us in the crew had this morning. And it was good. I would willingly sacrifice a couple of brews for an omelette like that. I think the Germans must have done a lot of this as the Arabs seem quite used to the business.

We have been issued with our K.D. (Khaki Drill) today, but have not yet surrendered our battle dress. It is different this year, bush jackets or shirts with the skirts worn outside the trousers and long slacks. If they fit decently, they should be quite smart.

13. 4. 43.

You had written your letter just as Rommel's withdrawal from the Mareth positions was announced. That was due to an error of judgement on his part, I believe. He held, as the French did when they built the Maginot line, that it could not be outflanked, but Montgomery has proved that they were wrong.

The positions - the geographical features in which they were built, rather - looked to my amateur eye as if they should have been impregnable. It is good to think that this time Rommel underestimated this British army. The boot has been too long on the other foot.

Since then a second battle has been fought and will, I believe, prove as decisive as Alamein. Here he seems to have been unprepared, not in actual preparations, but in where and when the attack was coming. I had a most interesting job in that do, but I'll have to leave the details until I see you.

One strange thing is slowly dawning on us. We had been used to a front of a hundred miles or more in breadth and of advances of fifty to one hundred miles a day. Now we are in a different country. It seems strange that the front at Akarit should be only ten or twelve miles wide and the advance slowed down to twenty-five miles a day. However, I wonder what the blokes from the western front in the last war would say of these conditions.

Another point about this fighting; at Alamein we felt that if ever there was a natural battlefield in the world, there it was. Nothing could make that piece of desert any worse. But now there are crops and olive groves and almost continuous habitation and agriculture and we have to be careful to do no more damage than is necessary. A tank across a cornfield is not a desirable thing.

I think the Arabs here must be living on next to nothing. Although there is much more cultivation than in Tripolitania and Cyrenaica, the Arab appears much poorer. Most of them are in rags and come begging for "mangeria" - food. We've had quite a number today already. Some of this is due to the poorness of the soil. But a good deal of it comes from indolence. They would much rather squat on their haunches and talk or doze than work.

Here is a little anecdote that may interest you. After the line at Akarit had fallen, we (our tank) was with a brigade H.Q. of the Highland Division. We had to go through the minefield at night and as you may remember, the Akarit business took place without a moon. The lane through the mines was very narrow and with some very awkward corners. It was impossible to see anything but the white tapes, which line such lanes, for about one yard only in front, and an occasional light which was put at a corner. Apart from this, the only things we saw were derelicts that had come to grief on the mines. The tank commander and I had our heads out of the turret as we crept through, and I don't mind admitting I went down in the turret on one occasion for a little prayer. Anyhow, we got through.

19. 4. 43.

In one of your letters, Evie mentions a raffle for half a dozen eggs. I'll make you thoroughly envious now. We've managed to get, between the four of us, forty eggs this week. We have been living very well. In addition to these eggs, one of our officers bought some sheep from an Arab and we had fresh lamb chops. They were rather expensive, worked out at about 3/- a head, but they were lovely. By great good luck, our rations had included some tinned peas that day and so we had lamb, peas and potatoes, followed by peaches. The whole day we did well, poached eggs on toast for breakfast, after oatmeal porridge; sardines at lunchtime, and that meal in the evening. The next morning we had liver and bacon too.

Today it is very hot and sticky. We had a little rain this morning just after we got up and it has promised more during the day. Yesterday, on the other hand, it was very hot in the afternoon. No one could say that the weather is settled.

When we first arrived in this spot, there was an Arab village of the tent variety within a hundred yards of us. They came over to see us almost immediately and apparently they didn't like the look of us. At dawn the next morning they packed everything up on their camels and moved, lock, stock and barrel. You know, it is all right if you can move like that when new neighbours come that you don't like.

We have had another change in our crew. The driver is now a lad from Tadworth near Epsom, a stockbroker's clerk in the city somewhere. He is a very decent lad and fits in well. He is twenty-two and has seen a good deal of service here. As you can imagine, when we are living as crews only four in number, it is very important that all get on well together. I should hate to be in a crew where there is any friction - thank God, I haven't yet.

I have mentioned Davies several times. He was the chap who got lost on guard. He is a sort of music hall turn in himself and can perform under almost any circumstances. Sometimes he is very witty, quite spontaneously. He is a rough diamond in many ways - really wicked, as he says himself - but he has a good heart and is easy to get on with. The fellows in the regiment are a good crowd, just as good as the old mob. I expect that is pretty universal in the army, though.

27. 4. 43.

Once again, I'm afraid I have gone a week without writing to you, but there has been no opportunity at all. We've made quite a long move and even if I had written, there would have been no chance to get it censored and off.

We are now once again alongside the Mediterranean. The scene of our camp is quite a picture postcard one - blue sea, white sand and palms. I'm sitting under a palm tree with the sea about two hundred yards away as I write this. The bathing is very good too, quite warm and with a sandy bottom. The night before last, we went in just before sunset and it was grand. By the time we were out, it was quite dark. It seems a pity that it has needed a war to give us these experiences.

The flowers here are more exotic perhaps in colour, but not really as pretty, and apart from the night-scented stock, I haven't come across any with a scent.

It seems strange to see the corn being reaped as early as May. We passed quite a lot being cut down. The women seem to do the main part of this work, as of all menial work. I was woken up this morning by the squeaking of a wheel on a well. It was only about fifty yards away. Once again, a woman was out with a cow harnessed to a rope and pulling water up. She was still doing this three hours later. They fill a sort of stone basin in front of the well, then let it out over the fields. There are shallow channels dug from the well and they just dam those where they want no water, and open those which lead to the parts to be watered today. It's just like all the textbooks have ever said.

There is another character to add to your collection. I've come across quite recently a chap named "Chips" Harris. We played bridge originally with him and that is how I met him. He is a corporal, but he only wears the stripes, he says, other people give the orders. He is a bank clerk, I believe, and looks older than he is, as he has a lovely walrus moustache. He is a complete character that wraps itself up in beautifully concocted phrases. Incidentally, he has the most atrocious luck at cards - always loses.

It's lunchtime - a sort of hors d'oeuvres; salad is being conjured up from the cold vegetables out of M and V, a sardine each and a boiled egg, purloined from the Arabs for sugar or tea or something.

CHIPS

Although I saw quite a bit of Chips during the summer of 1943, he is associated in my mind with one period alone - that of the forced march from the Eighth Army front to the First Army front in Tunisia.

During one of the enforced halts, four of us found time to play bridge and Chips was in the party. It was the first time I had met him - complete with walrus moustache and a string of phrases that were anything but platitudinous. When he had lost two or three rubbers, or whatever it was, he rolled out one which may not be polite, but was typically Chips. We had the luck of the "nine blind bastards". Such phrases came out naturally and I could never decide whether they were original or came from deep reading, for Chips was a cultured man.

This march was one of the most lovely experiences I had in North Africa. We had been knocking against the positions in the Enfidaville line for a fortnight or more with little success. It was then decided to switch some of the best divisions of the Eighth Army to the First Army front. This necessitated a very long march - two or three hundred miles, I believe - in order that we could take part in the final, triumphant manoeuvre that liberated Tunis.

I cannot remember passing through any villages between Kairouan and Le Krib, but the landscapes were some of the most beautiful I have ever seen. They appealed to me then, and I think hold a prominent place in my memory now, because they were like nothing else I have ever seen. The mountains were not high, at the most, two or three thousand feet. They were covered on their topmost slopes with pines, but they seemed to enclose bowls of the greenest grass or corn - it was May - that it is possible to imagine. We could creep over the crest of the track in the pass, and see before us one of these green bowls with the dark cone firs surrounding it. We would cross this bowl, climb up to the pass on the further side, creep over the crest once again and once again see before us a perfect, green bowl. And so the journey went on.

At one of the frequent halts we would climb a little way up the sides of the bowl and find that where there was no grass and yet no conifers, there would be the most perfect rock garden in creation. The commonest plant was the stone crop from the smallest kind, with minute leaves to a large variety, the bulbous leaves of which were an inch and a half long. The rocks were covered in the delicate colours of the rock-flowers.

Further on this journey, I felt it a little incongruous to see Arabs in galabiehs driving tractors.

Chips was at this time a technical storeman with sometimes as much as one inner tube to look after and he was travelling on a petrol lorry. Later he assumed the dignity of three stripes. Before his elevation, however, he had amused us all very much on a Brains Trust one night. We held a weekly session on the beach at Homs and it was a very popular programme. The questions ranged over the usual wide variety of topics and of course, included quite a number about the army. One which was never really satisfactorily answered was,

"If the Royal Navy and the Royal Air Force, why not the Royal Army?" Or in a lighter vein, "Where does 'all my eye and Betty Martin' come from?"

Chips completely silenced all venturers in reply to,

"Why does the Army not issue handkerchiefs, if it pretends to supply all wants?" with "The Army issues you all with a coat sleeve."

3. 5. 43.

I suppose it is a good thing that the public is more phlegmatic about success and reversals, but it doesn't mean, does it, that it is getting stale, is getting used to the war, whatever the fortunes may be. I hope that is not the case, as however smoothly the machine is working at home, it will always need just that little bit more to ensure that this thing is not interminable. I think it is true to say that we out here are still elated about success. Fortunately, we haven't had to put up with so many reverses in this campaign. Even the Mareth affair appears in a different perspective out here. We knew about the force that was attempting to out-flank the fortified line and so withdrawal didn't seem so desperate as it seemed over the wireless. The last stages seemed to be slow, but as long as some progress is being made, the situation is fairly satisfactory. Gerry has achieved one part of his objective in delaying us. I doubt if he can achieve the second part, in retaining a tip of the North African coast. Strategically, it seems to me, he must have a cut at doing this, as he could still dominate the central Med. from Sardinia, Sicily and Tunis.

There is a pretty stiff breeze blowing at the moment. It is a very welcome one, as the weather is getting pretty warm now. We have taken to K.D. and I rather like the outfit now - long slacks and a bush jacket - or shirt like a coat. It has to have a belt with it to look really smart. It is a very cool get-up and we've felt the benefit of it in the middle of the day. It is still cool enough in the early morning and the evening to wear a pullover or a greatcoat, however. And when I say early morning, I mean early morning. Reveille was at four-thirty this morning and has been at four-forty-five for a week or more.

Recently we have come through some of the most beautiful scenery I have ever seen, even including the Alps. It would be worth making the long journey just to see that alone. Ranges of mountains, grey at the top, tree covered on the lower slopes, with passes through and plains at the bottom of brilliant green wheat. Every time we cross one range, another valley shows itself, a little basin between the hills. There were streams trickling through, very much like Scotch burns, which is a strange sight for us after the desert. We find ourselves calling these wadis too, although they are not dry water-courses.

May 6/7th. The final attack on Tunis.

11. 5. 43.

This last week has been one of great exhilaration for us. At last the job which we began in October at Alamein is as good as finished. The last phase was dramatically quick too, like the last phase of the war will be. You have heard on the wireless or read in the papers, of our move right round to the First Army front and the attack we put in there. By four o'clock on the second afternoon, the tanks were in Tunis and we ourselves were on a hill only four miles west of it. It seemed incredible that the job had been done so easily. There have been crowds of Gerry prisoners too, most of them looking like first class troops. We have come across large dumps of material too. One was a food dump, with I don't know how much flour and tinned stuff in it.

I spoke to one young German prisoner. He was only twenty and a German-speaking Yugoslav. He said he had been waiting for a whole year for that day when he could give himself up as a prisoner. He'd only been over here twenty days - flew from Sicily. He was one of the lucky ones who did not find himself in the sea.

The people of Tunis have just gone crazy. One afternoon we pulled up in a village for a short stop and in about twenty minutes, they had brought out three bottles of wine and a pile of prunes for us. Another fellow passed down the column with a bottle of cognac. The French from the farmsteads round Tunis came out onto the road to clap and cheer, throw flowers at us and give the V sign. They all seem to use that.

Just imagine an English country lane, a woman going along the same way as we, suddenly turning round, throwing a kiss and shooting her arms up in the air with the screechiest "Victoire" imaginable. Or a quite staid, elderly man snatching off his beret and hurling it on the ground as we pass. But I expect if Hitler had invaded and a liberating army had been necessary, it would have thawed the stoniest and least emotional Englishman and received something of the welcome we got.

I went to Tunis yesterday and the scenes were quite indescribable. The streets were thronged with people and everyone was laughing, shouting and singing. Things were helped quite considerably by the freedom with which the wine was flowing; it is good wine but quite potent. Three of us gate-crashed, quite unintentionally, a party being thrown by the militia lads who have been here since the outbreak of the war. We were hauled in, a cup put in our hands and these kept pretty full. There was a French husband and wife there, with a boy aged ten, whom we talked to all the while. Or I should say, I talked to, as I was the only one of the three who had any French. All the nine years I spent at school at French were well spent if only for yesterday afternoon. I found I could chat fairly easily with a good deal of humouring from them. They were opticians from Bizerta when the Germans first came - on November 11th., and then moved to Tunis, only to be followed there. They said that conditions have been pretty bad. The lady had had no new clothes since the beginning of the war. Tea has just disappeared and cigarettes are almost unprocurable, and yet every woman in Tunis contrived to look smart. They also told us that the French who spoke English were put into concentration camps and these were actually freed yesterday morning.

Coming back through the streets, three fellows grabbed each one of us by the arms and walked along with us. The one I talked to went almost delirious when he heard we were from the Eighth Army. He said the Germans said the Eighth Army was as near invincible as possible. I've said before we are getting very swollen-headed and the events of the last week have not cooled us down very much.

15. 5. 43.

We can now reveal that we are part of the 22nd. Armoured Brigade and of the 7th. Armoured Division. You have already heard that it was our Brigade that was first into Tunis. The Eighth Army won the race after all. We did a very long march from the Eighth Army front to the First Army front, which took two days and two nights. Some of it was through the best scenery I have ever seen. Then we went in after the Indians on May 6th. At first we wondered how things were going, but by about midday we realised that all must be well, or rather better than well. We covered twenty miles or so that day and the remaining fifteen by four o'clock the next afternoon when Tunis came in sight. While we were on a hill overlooking the town, the 11th. Hussars were actually entering it. There was very little opposition really all the way along. I think the Gerries must have been surprised, and thought that we would push along the roads, instead of strike across the hills. We really didn't follow any valley, but went from ridge to valley and valley to ridge all the way. Anyhow, the job was over - or almost so, then.

Since, we have seen thousands and thousands of prisoners; 130,000 so far is the official figure, isn't it? It was amazing how quickly the German Army collapsed. I think they were very wise not to have attempted evacuation too, as very few would have got away. I think the end of the war will come as suddenly and dramatically as the end of the fighting did here.

We are just catching up a bit from the papers that are arriving now with the political muddle there was in N. Africa. It seems still that Giraud is officially to be regarded as the liberator. There are a number of his portraits stuck around Tunis, with just "Liberateur" under them. But also there are plenty of De Gaulle, Churchill and Roosevelt. The people all want to know where De Gaulle is and if Churchill and Montgomery will come to Tunis. They were very disappointed that Montgomery wasn't there as soon as the city fell. There are plenty of wall chalkings - "Viva De Gaulle", with the Lorraine cross, and V. Giraud held a parade the other day and seems to be in complete control of the whole of North Africa.

Incidentally, I saw him leaving the town. I wondered what was happening as I was standing at a crossroads. A policeman or an inspector of higher rank, came riding along pillion, on a motor bike, blowing a whistle and bouncing up and down on his seat. He got quite furious at the crossroads, but Giraud got through without any trouble. I'm afraid he hadn't the grace to acknowledge the cheers of the people in the streets, but sat talking to another general next door to him.

The Germans had treated these people very badly, hence their sense of freedom now. I suppose we are now learning for the first time, from first-hand experience, what German occupation means.

The soldiers were billeted in houses in the city, which had just been commandeered, whether empty or not. The French were most surprised when they learnt that we went to bed "en plein ciel". The Germans took everything they could lay their hands on. I heard two girls say yesterday that their rings were taken from their fingers by German soldiers as souvenirs. You can understand now why the wine flowed so freely when we arrived.

17. 5. 43.

As you can imagine, for a fortnight or more we have had little time for writing.

We visited the people we met in Tunis again in their flat. They seemed delighted to see us - "great honour you have paid us" and all that line of talk. They really made us very welcome, and produced a bottle of wine and talked away like mad. They told us more of the German occupation. The tales you have read are not exaggerated, I should say. Apparently, they live off the land at the expense of the local population and moreover, take anything they want from anywhere, commandeer a car on the road and leave the driver stranded, enter a flat and take a wireless or a carpet. They are just two of the incidents we heard about. The lad, aged about ten, made his first communion on Saturday and we were invited to the party.

One trouble is that there is little or no food in Tunis and it is virtually impossible to buy anything to eat. In time this will correct itself, I am sure, as there are very rich wheatlands around Tunis, and now this will not go to Germany or Vichy, but stay and feed the local population. The Gerries have put mines in some of the crops though; so reaping is going to be a ticklish job.

We have a canteen going again now, for the first time since Boxing Day, and it is a social venue in the evenings. We have been able to get quite a good supply of tobacco and cigarettes and some beer since coming to the First Army front, too. The atmosphere in the canteen at night is quite a happy one, as you can guess.

I've got another stamp to send you. This time it came from a letter in a German field post office. We came across thousands of letters in a ditch, all undelivered and unopened. We broke all confidences and had a look at one or two, both actually from Vienna, and in one, there was a string of stamps, which I put in my pocket. On the same spot was a huge food dump and a lot of equipment, including a brand new dental fit-up, folding chairs, basins and so forth, for a dental field centre.

29. 5. 43.

Once again, the speed with which the mail is travelling amazes me. After things taking so long, it seems strange that a letter you have written after the fall of Tunis should be here so soon. I should like to have been at home to witness the feelings there when the fall was announced. I don't know why the propaganda at home prepared everyone for a long siege of that corner of Tunisia. The fortifications were nothing like those at Mareth, which of course were taken because they were outflanked, or at Akarit, where there was a frontal assault. I saw very little evidence of strong fortifications behind Madjez where we started the last drive. I hear that the official view now of the collapse of the whole German army, is that the speed of our thrust was too much for Gerry to organise any resistance and he just flapped and his army became a shambles, which is very much what I said to you last time. Now we are having a rest in a very pleasant spot on the coast. We are parked down about two hundred yards from the sea, where the bathing is magnificent. We are among palms and so there is quite a picture postcard view. The chief snag is the high wind, which has blown the sand about quite a bit. May is the month of the Kamsin though, and so I suppose we can expect this for a week or so longer.

We can get into a town, a very small one, in the afternoons and evenings, if we want to. There is a cinema there, a Naafi one, and a small theatre for Ensa shows. An old Roman theatre that seats about five thousand is also being used for shows.

I paid a fleeting visit to Tripoli on Sunday as we were passing through. The place has improved greatly in the last three months, but there is still little to do. There are some cafés and bars open, but there is still only one cinema. I can't see it becoming much of a leave centre, as is intended, I believe.

You ask in your letter, about the countryside after the fighting has passed. Really, there was extremely little damage done. The worst I think was tank tracks through the corn and the burnt patches where our shells had fallen, but neither really were great. The Germans had not scorched the earth at all, as far as I know, which is very strange, as very valuable wheatfields are lost to them and regained by the allies.

The heaviest fighting was once again in the hills and rocky parts, where war can do little damage. Buildings, on the whole, were fairly intact. I saw one farm building demolished by twenty-five pounders, but only one. Some enthusiastic, but misguided Gerry infantry, saw fit to fight to the end although they were terrifically outnumbered, had tanks all round them and were soon within range of the guns, and consequently they were just blasted out. That was about eight miles from Tunis and was the only bit of destruction I saw.

The village Mareth, was a poor, pathetic place though. Practically every building was scarred somewhere. I think one reason why the people of Tunis were so glad to see us, was because they had feared the loss of all their crops and property in a siege, whereas in reality the whole thing was over before there could be any real fighting.

I see no harm in telling you now what that job at Akarit was. Our tank went off on its own to act as a liaison between the Highland Brigade which one squadron of our tanks was supporting, and the tanks themselves. We were at the Tactical H.Q. about three hundred yards the other side of the ridge, over which the fighting was happening. We couldn't see the actual battle, but could see the objectives, hills, of course, beyond and we heard a running commentary of the fight over the air. It was most interesting, a responsible job, but we managed satisfactorily. The Brigadier, a very fine man, complimented us the next day when the job was over. As the Gerries had started running and the regiment was chasing them, we stayed with the Highland Div. until Sfax. That was how we came to make a triumphal entry through Sfax a few hours after it had fallen. That night we spent with the Guards and a lot of our pre-conceived ideas about the Guards disappeared. No one could possibly have been more solicitous. We had three officers and the R.S.M. over to see we had everything we wanted.

2. 6. 43.

Since I wrote last week I have had quite a lot of mail. The registered letter of October 29th. turned up. This is over six months but I have cashed the orders. I had to sign an undertaking to return the money, if any claim had been made.

You said in one letter, I implied I'd been in action again. We have been hovering about on the edge of things really ever since the push on Tripoli began. For a long time at a time, of course, there was no real action, but then again things flared up at Mareth, Akarit, on to Sfax, the Enfidaville line, and the final push into Tunis. I saw yesterday the statistics. We came 2,225 miles from Alamein to Tunis at the average speed of 0.5 miles an hour! Anyhow, it is supposed to be the most rapid advance in the history of warfare. You will read into this, that in spite of being up with such a drive, it is possible to remain fit and happy and in most things contented; there were not many "ordeals" really.

You have probably read in the papers what a Scorpion tank* is and so you will now know what my old mob is doing. I must say I am very glad I changed now. The job this regiment has been given all the way from Marble Arch, is much more interesting and also I have made no end of really good pals. Jack Cole whom I've mentioned before, is a very good fellow and it has been good to get to know him alone. On the top of that, I feel that County of London Yeomanry means much more to me than a regiment which originated in Oldham. I hope I don't get mixed up in a re-shuffle again.

---

*A tank with flails to beat its way through minefields.

16. 6. 43.

We are still pretty busy here with the same occupations; sports, swimming and basket ball, bridge, the concert party and the wireless course. It seems that the test should be a week on Friday and so we are working from eight to one, with breaks of course. This seems a long time and I'm afraid we are not much use after twelve o'clock. After all, it is nearly midsummer, and although it is not as hot here as in the Delta or on the Suez, where we were last year, it is still pretty hot in the middle of the day. It can be quite cold at nights, though, and we usually throw a pullover over our shoulders at sundown.

The course should not be too difficult. The standard seems to be very much the same as the trade test I took fifteen months ago. The chief business is revision on the theoretical stuff and getting morse up to the requisite speed again. I've never used morse for all the time in between and am of course pretty rusty.

Last night we had a show in the camp given by a party from a neighbouring regiment. It was very good. One fellow sang a song which has been picked up from the German wireless. Apparently it is very popular with the German troops and a translation has been made that I think bids fair to becoming popular with us. It's Lili Marlene, I think that is how it is spelt. It reminded me very much of some of the German folk-songs we have heard them singing.

I am sorry this writing is even worse than usual. I've another sore on my elbow, within an inch of the other. It's an awkward place and needs a bandage to keep the dressing on. Consequently, it is difficult to bend my arm. Apart from writing and eating, I can't say it worries me much.

23. 6. 43.

The chief news this week is that we went out on a picnic for a couple of days to see the King. I really enjoyed them. In spite of a big parade, we were not worried by previous inspections and consequently found it a welcome break. We only saw him for a second or so as he drove by, sitting on the top of an open car. He looked quite tanned but very fed up. We afterwards learnt that he has had an attack of gyppy tummy and so I sympathise with him. It's bad enough if you've got comparative freedom, but if you've got to go through with a parade of that kind, it must be agony.

I admire him very much for coming out, particularly as it shows what control we have of the air. I don't know whether I've told you before, how little we have seen of the Gerry air force since Alamein. There were attacks there, sometimes by nine or fourteen planes, but never dangerous. Since then, I've really only seen two attacks. At Akarit, six came over just before sunset on the day of the battle, and dropped a bomb each, the nearest being two or three hundred yards off, and they were a sitting target. Four were shot down immediately. Then on the second morning of the Tunis push, three came swooping up over the ridge, again dropped one bomb each and fled. They did practically no damage, although someone told me they injured two German prisoners. Oh yes, there was another occasion just before Mareth, when they dropped one, about a quarter of a mile away, while we were having a Church service. In reality though, the German air force ceased to exist long before the army was beaten.

29. 6. 43.

It is terrifically hot today - most easily the hottest since last summer. The wind, still quite strong, has turned from the sea to the land and is of the Kamsin variety or "hot and scorching" as the guide books say. The best place is the sea.

This morning we passed very pleasantly, going to a cinema in a nearby town to see "Desert Victory". I'm glad we have been able to see this at last, as we had experienced so much of it ourselves. Except for one thing it was very true. The one thing was the tough tactics P.T. which we did not indulge in. I thought the shots before Alamein were better than the scenes of the battle. The life in the desert was so exactly right. I think the crash of the barrage at Alamein was a little theatrical. If I remember rightly, it took a couple of minutes to warm up and reach its peak and wasn't a sudden bang, from all thousand guns. Some of the shots were taken in this regiment and three or four people were quite clearly recognised. I thought also that the captured German films were quite telling.

7. 7. 43.

It has been extremely hot again since I last wrote. One day the shade temperature went up to one hundred and fifteen degrees and most days it has been over a hundred. At the moment it is about one hundred and eight and I am sitting in the shade of a palm tree with my back against it. We have changed our hours now so that we finish all training by ten-thirty. It is very much better that way. Of course, we get cooler in the sea, usually in the afternoon.

Last night we went to an "all star" variety show. The theatre, which holds five thousand, was absolutely packed and I had to stand up for the whole show. In spite of this, I thought it well worth while. The four principal attractions were Leslie Henson, Beatrice Lillie, Dorothy Dickson and Vivien Leigh. Vivien Leigh had obviously only been put in for her looks and sex appeal, and Dorothy Dickson is a bit heavy in the limb now for the kind of thing she does. But Leslie Henson is always good and Beatrice Lillie is outstanding, I think. I've only seen her two or three times, but she is in a class by herself. She did half a dozen or so character songs and they were extremely good. She hardly moves at all, but every time she does, it means something.

25. 7. 43.

I have been away from the regiment for a day's leave this week. We have to go some little distance, taking most of the morning. Then we leave about eight o'clock, do ten miles or so and bed down by the side of the road, finishing the journey the next morning. It's the first time since we came that I have done it, and although the journey is a bit of a bore, it makes a change and one gets away from the regimental atmosphere for twenty-four hours.

When once there I enjoyed myself. There wasn't a lot of time and we had tickets for a show. We attempted to do a little shopping, not very successfully, I must admit, and we had a gharry ride! The show was an Ensa one and very good, slick and polished, which will carry any show through. Really, these Ensa shows are more like isolated variety turns, than the good old fashioned concert party. There was a very good comedian in a style of his own.

Apart from that the week has been much as usual. The Brains Trust on Thursday was quite a success again. It is quite an institution now after only two sessions. We have now by us some thirty or forty questions carried over from these two weeks and so can work them in if necessary in the future. The whole business needs some stage-management, selection of the questions and the right order, for example, but it is certainly a very easy way of providing an hour and a half's profitable entertainment for as many as like to come.

It's pretty warm again now, the temperature in the region of one hundred and ten degrees, I should say. I'm writing this quite early in the morning before it gets really hot and sitting under a palm tree. There is a very pleasant breeze blowing. In the heat of the day, this breeze will get so hot that it will be one of the most unpleasant features, searing and parching.

8. 8. 43.

I'm sorry that I missed writing as usual on Wednesday, but just about then, I was having a bit of a tussle with a microbe left behind by a lady mosquito - it's the first time I remember being bitten by the female of the species! Anyhow, at the moment I'm reclining in bed in hospital with malaria. I hope - I think at least - that the most unpleasant part of the trouble has passed, but how long it will take to effect a cure I don't know.

I first felt queer last Sunday, but then it was not too bad. On Tuesday I was sick and went to the M.O., who found I had a pretty high temperature. Strangely enough, I had no aches or pains, however high the temperature rose. They got rid of me from the unit and eventually I finished up here, and for the first time for ten months, I find myself between sheets. I'd almost forgotten how to use a bed, I realised on the first night. It rather looks as if I shall be spending my birthday in hospital or a convalescent camp. If I go on like this, I shall feel a complete fraud most of the time.

12. 8. 43.

I left hospital yesterday, for a convalescent depot where I am continuing the treatment. This will go on for nine days or so and so I expect I shall be here for the best part of a fortnight. The treatment, now that I have been completely saturated with quinine, seems to consist of taking tablets three times a day. I suppose that is to kill the wretched little microbes. Incidentally, I understand that the particular type of malaria I have, is non malignant, that is, it won't recur once I am cured of this bout. That is good to know as I don't fancy having a dose or two a year for the rest of my life.

It is a week now since I last had a temperature and I am not feeling too bad at all. In fact, except when I had a high temperature - for about four hours each afternoon for three days, I haven't really felt ill.

20. 8. 43.

Once again I'm writing to you from the convalescent depot. I'm on my last day of treatment today and so hope to be out fairly early next week and also to rejoin the regiment within a day or two of leaving. I've spent a very lazy week, but quite a pleasant one, doing little else but reading. In spite of that I shall be glad to get back to the fellows again.

Jack Cole and a chap named Cordery came in to see me this morning. This last chap was driver of our tank way back in January. The other day our troop officer, Murray Gladstone, and the Padre turned up to see how I was, very good of them I thought, as they had made a fifty or sixty mile journey to do it.

I think I remember saying last year, I wondered where I would spend my birthday next year. I little thought it would be in a convalescent depot getting over malaria.

There is an education centre here. I've been along three nights this week. What really made me go was the announcement of a talk, "My reminiscences as a schoolmaster". The next night it was Play Reading and last night once again, a discussion on education, which mostly hinged round the raising of the school leaving age.

29. 8. 43.

I'm back again with the regiment now and very glad to be. It's taken just about a month to get the whole job over, as it's exactly four weeks today since I was first bad.

I had a good piece of luck when I left the convalescent depot. One goes to a transit camp to wait for transport back to the regiment. I had hardly been there ten minutes before Hugh Bishop walked into the tent. He had been slightly wounded in Sicily, a little piece of shrapnel in the arm - and was quite better. The next day another fellow from the old mob came in and the third day yet another. He was with the Scorpion tank crowd. I heard quite a lot about the fellows I haven't seen since November. It was a very good piece of luck to bump into them.

That business about a Scorpion. I can definitely assure you that a Scorpion goes through all the motions of raising its tail over its head and stinging and it dies almost immediately afterwards. Why it dies, I leave to the experts. The ones I've seen here have been about one and a half to two inches long. Their bite is not fatal, but just causes swelling of the limb and sometimes of the body. If you can get a grain of permanganate of potash into the sting almost at once, there is no reaction at all. But in point of fact, I've never heard of anyone being stung! We usually discover them and do the ring of fire stunt. I say usually. We have done it three times in these last three months. I'm certain they are not nearly as great a danger as the common fly which is becoming a very great pest again.

BISH

I met Bish on my first day in the army. I had gone, not inexperienced in life, because I had packed a fair amount into my thirty-three years, but raw in military matters, although I had served in a school O.T.C., to an R.A.C. training regiment at Catterick. The other fellows in my squad looked, much as any other eighty would, drawn from all walks in life and placed together suddenly in a couple of barrack rooms. Later I discovered most of them to be fellows of sterling worth and when the time came for splitting, there were many who thought that we should never again in the army achieve as close a companionship.

On that first day I found in the next bed to me, a lad who was obviously a student. He wore the orthodox grey flannels and tweed sports coat; he was big, rather ungainly and very much a boy to look at. I soon discovered, that night, I think, that he was reading History at Oxford; he had no real decision on his future career, although he inclined towards anthropology; was distinctly red in his political views and took the view that while Russia could do no ill, the British Government very seldom could make a wise decision; read voraciously; loved and understood good music; in short was an intelligent, if somewhat immature thinker. And as I also read History at one time, was a little red, even though much more moderate, now professed English as my subject, and also appreciated "highbrow music," it was not extraordinary that Bish and I soon knew each other very much better.

At Catterick we passed the same wireless course together. After four months we were posted to the same service unit together. There we took a second wireless course together. Finally, within nine months of joining the army, we found ourselves on the same troopship together, bound for some destination unknown. On the boat Bish and I spent quite a large part of the time avoiding the incredible crowds of troopships by playing bridge. He had known very little of the game when I first met him, but from my meagre knowledge he picked up one or two more points and most afternoons would find him and me and two others, trying to make ourselves as comfortable as possible on the deck and playing a rubber. As it was during the early summer that we left England, and even the southern winter is like the English spring, the weather was highly suitable and a game on deck most enjoyable. Far different was it when we returned in midwinter and when our Bridge, not with Bish, alas, this time, was played on the tables of crowded mess-decks with objecting comments against bridge schools from all sides. I was very glad to introduce him to Toc H on the boat too. I found among the troops three padres, who had known Toc H in peace and together we fixed up a meeting. To our surprise there were some thirty members on board and another twenty who were interested enough to attend. Bish was one of these. I knew he had ideals for building a better world, but I did not know how he related these ideals to his religious beliefs, if he had any. Apparently Toc H helped him to relate his thoughts in these subjects, as he was "bitten" at once and became an enthusiastic supporter of the movement.

But it was in South Africa that Bish and I shared experiences alone. Both in Capetown and Port Elizabeth we were entertained, the two of us, by the most charming people. I felt at the time, a little ashamed, that at home there was no welcome for troops to compare with that in South Africa. I had been lucky myself. At Eastbourne for example, I had met a family which I am glad to number among my most intimate friends now, and what a relief it is to get away from khaki into a real live family! These friends even thought it worthwhile to visit my parents when I had, through force of circumstances, not written to them for a long time. But on the whole, such friendships formed between soldiers and the civilians among whom they are billeted are rare. In South Africa, however, the fellow who did not make friends was the exception. Bish and I went to Table Mountain one afternoon. I suppose the view from the sea is the finest. We saw it the first time when we went on deck early one morning. We were approaching it with the sun just rising behind it and a beautiful silhouette it appeared. Along the east, the mountainous coast line of almost conical peaks, contrasted strangely with the flatness of the Table Mount itself. From the harbour too it appeared grand, perhaps more grand because it rises so unexpectedly from the city itself. But Bish and I wanted to see the mountain at close quarters and if possible to go to the top.

Unfortunately the wind at the head of the cable railway was too strong and we had to content ourselves with a walk along the terrace at the bottom of the railway. I remember seeing here, for the first and only time, a dossie or rock rabbit asleep on a crag. We walked back to the main road, and, having just made up our minds to explore away from Capetown, we were stopped by a gentleman in a car overtaking us. His cheery invitation to join him could not be resisted, even if we would. He and his sister took us to Camp's Bay, a charming little spot, where we had tea. Then followed one of the best rides I have ever taken. We drove underneath these conical peaks which we had seen from the sea. The Twelve Apostles, they are called. From the more distant end, Table Mountain contrasts in yet a new way with the nearer mountains. The coast line, as that of Italy did later, reminded me of Cornwall, but it is wider, grander, more open, which of course, is just as it should be in a new country. That afternoon our return journey took us through Constantia and the vineyards. I know now where the South African vines originate and in what surroundings. While in Capetown the atmosphere is one of recent growth, of tall, modern rectangular buildings mixed up with what might well be settlers' shacks, in the Constantia vicinity there is an air of age and tradition. Most of the farmhouses are Dutch in type and several are genuine "ancient buildings". We stopped just after dark on the terrace of the New University and watched the lights of Capetown. The twinklings of a large city after dark, particularly if there is water there, have always fascinated me since the time when I spent hours watching those of London, from a house on Blackheath Hill. Now two years of black-out at home gave these a greater fascination still. The main roads, Adderley Street, for example, stood out as long straight lines of lights. The suburban districts were terraces of lights, the harbour shimmering reflections.

On another day, these new friends took us to Muizenberg and Fishbay. Bish and I were attracted to flamingos on the flats of False Bay but strangely enough, they looked more out of place here in their natural surroundings, than they do in St. James's Park. They are an ornamental bird and need an ornamental setting.

We talked for a long time to our friends in South Africa. Our host told us much of the general trend of South African politics. Everyone whom we had met had expressed relief at the fact that Smuts had won, even by so small a majority, the general election at the beginning of the war. Everyone also expressed nothing but disgust at the Ossewa Brandewach or the O.B.'s, the pro-German nationalist party, which was by this time largely discredited.

We also discussed with him the apparent lack of an indigenous culture in South Africa. Books, magazines, and periodicals seemed mostly to come from England or America. It was my impression too that the majority came from the United States. Films were almost exclusively American. Even the dramatic art seemed starved. Although (while we were there) there was an operatic week in Capetown, in which the Capetown Orchestra and an amateur chorus and ballet gave very adequate performances, we were told that this occasion was the first such for two years. When we expressed the opinion that it should have been relatively easy in an opulent country like South Africa for local arts to flourish, our host agreed, but left us with the impression that nothing very much could or would be done about it. Bish and I left Capetown with a fine impression of the new country if only built up during a few days' stay.

This impression was further imprinted on our consciousness after we had spent about as long in Port Elizabeth. Here again we met a charming family with a musical inclination. Bish and I spent an evening in their house enjoying home-made music, which was as near to any South African culture that we approached.

I associate Bish with this part of my army experience for two reasons. First, he and I found ourselves alone more often than not in South Africa. Secondly Bish, more than anyone I have met in the army, possessed a mind that was eager for new ideas. He was constantly anxious to find out new facts for himself, particularly about politics, and it was therefore good to be with him in South Africa.

Bish appears again at Alexandria. Not that he had really disappeared. I had seen him every day since landing, except for a short period during the battle of Alamein, when he had gone into first line reinforcements. But after Alamein, we found ourselves back for a period in Alex, and once again Bish and I always seemed to be in the party.

We used most extensively the clubs of the city and if South Africa could set a standard of hospitality in homes, the European communities in Egypt can set a standard of the organisation of service clubs. The Springbok (semi-official), the United Forces, the Minora, the Britannia, the Jewish Club, Y.M.C.A., Talbot House, Wesley House, are only a few of these and each seems to have agreed to cater for one branch of the service man's needs. The United Forces Club provides dinners with waiters, a most welcome feature to men who have queued for months for their meals. Then also there are baths, barbers' saloon, and lounges, and in the garden a large tessellated dance-floor. The Britannia Club, although it serves light meals, is best known for its second floor, which is exclusively a library. The rooms are most comfortably furnished and the walls lined with books, both furniture and books mainly loaned by the British community, I believe. Of course it is not possible to borrow the books, but Bish and I spent many hours dipping into the shelves here. The Y.M.C.A. club's unique attraction is the nightly "Music for All". I am not at all sure that the title adequately describes the hour's programme. It is really "Music for the discerning few", but where there are so many troops as in Alexandria, the few are quite numerous. Programmes that I heard ranged from Beethoven's Choral Symphony to Holst's "Planets". I wonder if it would not be possible here at home for the various committees of canteens in any one town, to get together and work out some sort of agreement.

The Y.M.C.A., also run sight-seeing trips round Alex, but Alex is not Cairo. I enjoyed mooching round the old and native parts of Cairo but there are really only two ancient sites in Alex, Pompey's Pillar and the Catacombs. The former is uninteresting, but the latter is most fascinating. I suppose it is morbid to visit underground cemeteries, but it was the first such place I had seen. The mere fact that it was cut out of the solid rock, for eighty feet below the surface of the ground made it singular, but the carvings on the altars of Isis and Osiris and Hoth and the other Egyptian Gods made it unique in my experience. The anthropological in Bish showed itself on this visit.

He was also intrigued by the Coptic Church. A little lad of eleven or twelve showed us round with the help of two or three other of his school-mates. All wore red fezzes inside the Cathedral. We asked them why they wore fezzes at all as they were not Moslem and they merely shrugged their shoulders and said, "Everyone does." We asked if they found any different treatment because they were Christian and they replied that no government appointments would be open to them, but they seemed to take this lack of tolerance as inevitable. Although they were most particular in pointing out that we could not enter the sanctuary, they showed little reverence for the reliquary of St. Mark. The Cathedral has a casket which is supposed to contain one of his fingers. The self-appointed guide, picked up the casket and rattled it to prove to us that there really was a finger inside. There is also an elaborate cross presented by Haile Selassie, also a member of the Coptic Church. But the most interesting point in the decoration of the church was the lack of images and the pictures, which appeared to take their place. These pictures of the saints were painted on the wooden screens which completely cut the nave from the chancel, and were mostly of the saints. The haloes, however, and in the case of St. Mark the gospel, were of beaten gold.

Yet another of Bish's cravings was satisfied during this short stay near Alex. The Palestine Symphony Orchestra paid the Delta a visit and gave two concerts for the troops in Alexandria. The first was by the string section of the orchestra, quite small in size, but exquisite in craftsmanship. The second was by the "light section" and played more popular works. It appears that the Middle East can develop its own culture where South Africa fails.

After these few weeks in Alex, Bish and I were separated, he being posted to a unit "east of Suez," and I to one well west. It was some eight months before our paths crossed again. Any meeting in the desert or under service conditions must be completely fortuitous and always happens when it is least expected. I had allowed myself to be bitten by a female of the species and had a dose of malaria. Bish had gone to Sicily in the original invasion party and had been wounded slightly by shrapnel in the forearm. We both were cured and went to a transit camp, to await such time as we could get back to our units. I arrived by truck one afternoon and had only just found a tent to sleep in, when Bish loomed in the doorway. He had been in the camp about three days then.

I only remained "in transit" for two days, but most of that time was spent with Bish. The conditions of a transit camp are not ideal for meeting an old friend. There were at this time between three and four thousand in the camp; the meal queues had to be seen to be believed; there was no privacy of any kind. So Bish and I spent most of the time on the shore of a little bay, just talking.

I returned to the regiment and within four days had left again, this time to collect tanks for the Italian adventure. We went to a spot some eight kilometres from Tripoli and were able to visit it several times. Bish was still waiting to return to his unit, but as it meant a sea-trip to Sicily, his departure was somewhat indefinite. I saw him a number of times, just the same old Bish, a bundle of books under his arm and making his way to a recital. These recitals in Tripoli were held in the "Parish Church". The Church, had, I imagine, been the dinner-dance room of a hotel. It was semi-circular in shape, with a stage, a parquet floor, small alcoves and balcony. The decorations were most modern in style. But the padre had transformed the dance-hall into one of the most attractive churches I have ever seen. The colours of the hangings were grey and pink, almost natural the furniture (given by parishes in England) and the lighting was most diffuse. Here there was a daily recital of gramophone music.

I also went to the Toc H House with Bish; in fact, we did all the old things together.

There must be a postscript to this sketch. I have heard that Bish died of wounds in Italy on December 7th. 1943.

9. 9. 43.

The news last night of Italy's surrender was good, but not unexpected. I gave it a week after the first troops landed. This knock out blow is going to be a terrific affair and, I hope, so well prepared that there is no possible chance of failure. We have learnt that the success of the Eighth Army was due to this long and careful planning. Only once in the whole N. African campaign, did the Army H.Q. temporise, when it sent an armoured division round in the outflanking move at Mareth, after Gerry had counter-attacked and got back most of the ground. That of course was the only temporary reverse we had. The Mareth plan was being considered before we took Tripoli. The major European offensive must have even more planning than this.

Yesterday I had an hour or two in town. I had a haircut and shampoo and was horrified and thoroughly ashamed to see the result. The scalp must have had a thick layer of sand on it. Then I managed to get a dinner, not frightfully Frascati, but at least I had it off a tablecloth. Then again to a gramophone recital; the main work was Grieg's Piano Concerto. They must have been old records as the artists were Arthur de Greef and Sir Landon Ronald. The reproduction was excellent though, and it was grand to hear some good music again.

I see when I wrote the letter you were answering, that I had that desert sore. It is still there and has been joined by two or three others. I had one that developed in hospital but that cleared up perfectly last week. I hope this does as quickly. Every time I bark my hands in this God-forsaken country, I'll have one. A couple of days without sand would put them right - and without flies too.

ITALY

SEPTEMBER - DECEMBER 1943.

C.M.F.   25. 9. 43.

You will see from the address that the move you have been speculating about for so long has come about. We had a very pleasant trip over - quite like a sea cruise. I could have done with one twice as long. The sea was like a mill-pond all the way, and of course, there was the brilliantly sunny Mediterranean weather.

Since we have actually landed, we have made the most of the fresh fruit and vegetables. We are in an orchard at the moment with plenty of apples and walnuts ready to eat, oranges nearly ripe, a huge field of tomatoes on our right and out left quite a lot of grape vines. I think we must have eaten about two lbs of tomatoes a day and they have had their effect already. The desert sores are disappearing. I barked my shin on the boat and the next morning it had come up yellow. Today however, there is a healthy red scab on it. I should have thought the vitamins and what-not would not have had quite so quick a result.

About half way through this, I went off in search of potatoes. We heard that there were some about but we were not very successful. We got a lot more walnuts, some much riper oranges and also some corn-cobs. It doesn't look as if we are going to be short of fresh food-stuffs, which will be a great change. I am going to make some orangeade of the oranges. I've already made some lemonade and it leaves Kia Ora standing.

26. 9. 43.

I am now in Italy. You have been wondering long enough where I was and if I was in Europe. Now you need speculate no longer. I always felt from the time of leaving home that I would return via Italy and it looks as if that is what will happen. Anyhow, I hope I don't go back to North Africa.

We came over on a Yank tank landing craft. We were not particularly crowded, as we were on the troopship coming out, which helped the pleasantness of the journey. We (our crew) pulled up with a couple of the crew, two very nice fellows. They were mad on souvenirs. Unfortunately, the only thing I had was a German infantry belt I got from a prisoner at Tunis, but they were thrilled with that. In return, they were very generous with us, and gave us a dollar note as a souvenir, a couple of pounds of sweets, six loaves of bread (we are back on biscuits of course), a couple of packets of Edgeworth tobacco, which I believe is considered one of the best American tobaccos, and a pipe, which I am smoking at the moment. I think we all got on very well with the Yanks, in spite of what Lord Haw-haw would wish you to believe.

We had quite a job getting on to the beach. It took us ten hours and six attempts. The boat was really too heavy, I think, and grounded a little way out each time. The trouble with the Mediterranean is that there isn't sufficient tide to sit back and wait for deeper water. It doesn't come up more than two or three feet. The navy worked very hard putting up a smoke-screen, with the result that only four shells came over us in the ten hours and they were nowhere near.

My tank commander has changed again. He is now a South African who volunteered for active service. He is in many ways one in a million, just mucks in with us completely and is not afraid of doing the heaviest work. He manages this a darned sight better than any of us do. Everyone here is most affable at the moment - all the officers and the R.S.M., whose tank is alongside us.

Our job promises to be interesting too. We are the Colonel's protection - he is now Lord Cranley, son and heir of the Earl of Onslow. We are part of his battle H.Q. I'm now his no. 2 operator and although I don't anticipate it, if anything happened to his operator

I should have to take his place. Operators come in for far more work in an H.Q. troop than in a fighting squadron. There are wireless watches during night and day, when most sets are closed down. Then there is liaison work to do and that kind of thing. It is of course much more interesting than the other sorts of work.

1. 10. 43.

You will know by now that I have been back in the regiment for some time and have fully recovered from the bout. All that remains now is to take precautions against another dose. We sleep under nets whenever possible, put anti-mosquito cream on the exposed parts of our bodies and the most important thing, I think, take tablets at night which will suppress the diseases, should we be bitten.

You would be interested in the people here. They are very poor in type. The peasants are little better, if at all, than the Arabs. They are bare-footed and their clothes consist of the most conglomerate mixture of patches you could imagine. The better class are none too well dressed or cleaner either. The folk round here have been without food for three weeks now. There is an abundance of fruit but the Germans took all supplies and even raided private houses. All the tales we hear show that the Germans are treating Italy just like an occupied country. We stopped opposite a shop which had been looted by ordinary German soldiers.

We seem to be quite popular. As soon as the Ities hear we are English, they don't mind. Strangely enough they have quite a different opinion of the Americans. I was wandering with Jack Cole in an orchard and the fellow there tried to shoo us out, but when we didn't go, he came up to us with half a dozen peaches and asked us if we were English. When we said "Yes" - (si, si, si,) he smiled, saluted us and walked away. We were warned that we should probably make ourselves too amiable.

Sometimes I feel sorry for the people cringing for food, or to see the houses wrecked - the main road to Salerno is pitiful - but then I think, you asked for it, you came into the war at a time when you thought you could invade our country and bring all this mess there. I get quite hard then, only to soften when we pass another wrecked house.

7. 10. 43.

You have probably heard tales about the atrocities the Germans have been committing in Italy and possibly taken them as propaganda. I am writing this NOW to let you know you can believe anything you read. We are all aghast at what we've seen and heard.

(I leave out details of the atrocities which I wrote about in the letter as they are recorded later in the account.)

We have had no end of tales which we can't vouch for ourselves, the Germans throwing hand-grenades into windows as they drove by in retreat and so on, robbing people in the street of their clothes and shoes, doing the Chicago gangster stuff in shops, killing all sheep and cattle and taking it along with them. Certainly yesterday we saw sheep for the first time since landing, when a large flock was brought out an hour or so after we had cleared the village. Another fellow was digging up his wireless set and accessories, as we passed, as it was "bono" now. We had a very good jug of wine from him.

You can imagine with what relief the folk have seen us come into their little towns and villages. We had a welcome in Tunis and it is just as warm here. Every village is thronged with people clapping us as we go through, in a queer way because they clap over their heads. I believe they are genuine, although the Italians are supposed to be fickle, but after the terrors of the last three weeks, I can't see how it can be anything else but genuine. In one village there was chalked up on a piece of paper,

"Hurrah for Liberty, Hurrah for the Liberators, Welcome to you!" So it looks as if our propaganda has got across and they do look on us as liberators. Anyhow I think we all feel we are doing a worthwhile job.

We have been snowed under with fruit. We had to leave behind a large sackful of apples yesterday when we moved on a bit. We've had baskets of these and walnuts pushed on us. We had to take them for fear of offending. Today we are by an orchard with some of the sweetest and finest apples I have ever tasted. At times a chap will climb up on the tank and give us cognac or liqueur or wine.

There are a few who speak English. They all seem to have learnt it in New York. They all say how pleased they are to see the English

again. One dear old mamma spoke it just like the burlesque version on films and when we went, she said,
"Gooda bye and Goda blessa you."

10. 10. 43.

I think the chief item of interest this week is the party we went to the other night. The previous night the rest of the crew had been invited in by some Italians and then to dinner the following night. We provided the meat stuff out of our rations and they cooked it and the vegetables. I don't know quite who was there. There seemed to be masses of people from three families. Anyhow twenty-two were fed somehow. They lived in a typical Italian house. They seem to be built round a courtyard with a balcony.

The oven was outside in the courtyard and when we arrived, Mamma was sitting at a brazier outside the front door turning over chipped potatoes.

The farms apparently hold everybody. I slept two nights in a room in one. Once again the buildings were built round a courtyard, entered by a massive gate in a high wall from the street. There was a balcony also. There seemed to be a number of families of the farmer and his hands living in the various rooms. Incidentally, these are the first two nights I've slept under a roof since October 1st. last year when I went to Cairo.

The whole of this part of S. Italy is very squalid. A family - enormous in size - lives in one room. There is a huge bed, which you can see through the front door as you walk down the street. There is also usually a huge sideboard on the other side of the room, and in between a table and sewing machine or cobbler's bench or whatever they earn their living by. Perhaps this is due to overcrowding as there are a number of refugees from Naples in these parts. I feel certain though that overcrowding is the order of the day, as families of eight or ten seem usual. Most women seem to have a child of nine or ten months in their arms and another obviously on the way.

I suppose I'm missing a lot of sights that a tourist in Italy would be shown, but I am certainly seeing a lot Mussolini wouldn't have liked advertised. It is difficult to see what he has done for these village communities.

20. 10. 43.

We've had a busy day today and an interesting one too; I only wish I could tell you what my particular job today has been, but it is much too much mixed up with the present operations, both in place and material, not to be a most serious breach of security, if I disclose it.

I got back with the driver, (only the two of us were out), to find the other two members of the crew had cooked a chicken, and so we had chicken, onions, peas and potatoes for dinner.

The chicken came from our tank commander, the South African who has been away from us for about a week now on another job. He is not far away, only about a mile, but where he is, he found a number of chickens not being looked after as the civilians had naturally evacuated, and also, an empty chicken run. So he rounded them all up into the pen and is feeding them on scraps. When he called in to see us yesterday, he promised us a couple, which turned up today. So we still have another for tomorrow. He also promised us a pig which is going spare up there. Fortunately, our driver is a butcher in civvy street and can cope with such things.

For the first time since I have been out here, we are finding buildings to sleep in. We had a couple of good nights in farmhouses and thought we were good for a third in a police building, but it developed a nasty crack just after we had settled down to sleep, and we thought our tanks were safer.

You've heard about the rain in Italy recently and, believe me, there has been plenty. Fortunately the sun is fairly hot when it comes out and dries things up quickly. The worst part really is the mud. We've got our winter clothing now, including gaiters, and I'm very glad to wear them.

30. 10. 43.

I went to a little town yesterday and managed to get you a dress length again for Christmas. I think too it is better material than last year.

This town - quite important in a way - was once again a typical South Italian place, filthy, smelly and squalid. I suppose if they were really cleaned up, they could look attractive, but they certainly don't at the moment. This one seemed to have escaped most of the effects of the war, but it still didn't appeal. The shops are very little better than the Arab shops in Cairo or Tripoli, just a small room with a door butting on the street and perhaps minute windows or show cases on each side of the door. They have little or no stock at all, but I suppose that is due to the war.

The people, as I have said before, fit these surroundings well. I think there are more craftsmen than you would see at home - in each village you go to there are two or three blacksmiths. There are cobblers sitting at open doors, tailors with their sewing machines almost on the road, harness menders and so on. That is because life is more primitive. It seems funny that the higher the standard of living, the less craftsmanship there is about.

The women too are treated very much like the Arab women. They seem to do all the work; the other day I saw one carrying a treadle sewing machine on her head.

Two of the other members of the crew have seen that family we had dinner with again. I didn't tell you that when we left the village to go into action again, they were most upset. I think they saw us all as corpses. The girls wept at once and as we left even the fat old papas had tears in their eyes. Yesterday when these two arrived, the whole crowd was madly excited. It appears there were three families living there, all evacuees from Naples, and they are returning to Naples quite soon. I suppose they must have confidence in the British A/A. There have been only a few raids on Naples, only two I've seen anything of, but from this distance the barrage looked like Brock's firework display at Crystal Palace. I don't think many planes could get through it. The second night two bombers were brought down near enough for us to see, both by night fighters, and within five minutes of each other.

At the moment I am doing a spot of wireless instruction. There are a number of fellows, mostly sergeants, from another regiment who are coming to us to pick up what we know. It's the first bit of teaching I have done for over two years and strange though it may seem, I am quite enjoying it. Of course we don't have classes of forty for one thing. The most you get in the army is six to eight, and for practical stuff like working the wireless, you only get two.

Now we are more settled, I've been seeing more of Jack Cole. We are in railway trucks and he and another fellow, who isn't often in, have dug themselves nicely into a passenger compartment. Incidentally, the trains have been wrecked, seats slit, windows broken by Gerry before he left. I have spent each evening with Jack in his abode since we have been here, and it has been very pleasant. Last night, we indulged in building castles in the air, as we lay imbibing a bottle of Vermouth.

2. 11. 43.

We arrived when the Salerno battle had turned in our favour - I've forgotten the date myself. We had a day out on Sunday and I thoroughly enjoyed it. We went first to Pompeii and then back to Naples. I badly wanted to see Pompeii when we first came up, but of course there was no chance. I wasn't at all disappointed in the ruins although I've heard and read so much about them. It's a little uncanny too, to walk along the narrow roads just as they were 2,000 years ago, by the side of ruts in the stone worn out by the chariots, for example. I think they must have been a standard gauge, like the railway trains. The town seems to have been a very wealthy place for pleasure only. The houses are large, what is left of the decoration pretty sumptuous and there seem to have been any number of bars. In one corner of the town are still left some frescoes which are far cruder than the most pornographic pictures on sale in Cairo, for example. I believe the rooms are normally closed, but I suppose it is considered that the soldier's mind can be polluted no further.

Naples is worth visiting, I suppose, but I have seen much finer cities. The bay must have been beautiful, but the front itself is a mass of docks and railway lines. The Bay is almost enclosed by mountains of which Vesuvius is one. The city itself has been knocked about a good deal near the docks, but only isolated buildings seem to have been hit apart from that. Practically every shop within half a mile of the shore has suffered from blast. I was told the General Post Office had had a block-buster in it, but the shell is still standing.

It's not fair to judge a city in conditions like these, of course. I expect in summer in peacetime it was a very beautiful place. There is a long road of high-class shops, not large, more like Bond Street. Unfortunately on Sunday they were closed.

Old Vesuvius keeps on the go. There is always a cloud coming from him and at night you can see a shower of red ashes shoot up about every ten seconds.[*] On the way up, I did a guard underneath Vesuvius one night and had plenty of opportunity to study him. It's rather like Crystal Palace and the dust destruction chimney at home. It seems impossible to lose him.

---

[*]Vesuvius last erupted in March 1944.

14. 11. 43.

You will have noticed that I give you no details of anything until months after the event - that is the way of action. But as I've said before, when you try to guess what I'm doing, you almost invariably would be wrong. Jack Cole and I made that remark on Friday about one o'clock. You would never have guessed that we were sitting down in a restaurant on the waterfront at Naples, boats of all kinds in front of us, an ancient castle built on an island to the right, and eating a very good lunch and drinking a very good wine. We had another day in the city and found this place for lunch. The food was more plentiful than we had found elsewhere and very tasty. The fish course was roast tunny. We have had this tinned and it was very salty and tough. But fresh and roast it was delicious. There was the inevitable trio there, violin, guitar and tenor, and they played and sang several pieces to us. Jack Cole wanted some Strauss and in the middle of it, asked the singer. He turned to the violinist and said, "Strauss," the violinist turned to the guitar and repeated, "Strauss," and the guitarist stopped the piece he was playing and went into the boomp boo boo, boomp boo boo of the Blue Danube.

Naples is quite quickly getting as near to normal as possible. There are quite a lot of Ities working on the roads to clear up the air-raid damage and get the communications working again. The trams of course stopped when Gerry blew up the power station. They did stop just at that moment too, and are in the most awkward places, on corners and so on. There is a cinema going too, although I don't know where they get the power from. I believe a theatre is opening for the troops tomorrow.

23. 11. 43.

I have told you of our recent move[*]. At the moment I am sitting in a quiet room and acting as librarian in between writing to you. The fellows all seem to need a good deal of help in choosing what to read. We have managed to get together a pretty good library now. These are packed away in boxes when we are on the move, but at the moment they are in a typical schoolroom cupboard, which I quite blatantly looted from an elementary school in which we have our billets. I also won from the same place a sort of reading desk, on which I put the newspapers in true library style. I say newspapers, although I have had only one edition yet - there is a British newspaper published in Naples now.

I've got some pictures on the walls. They are home-made affairs but they brighten the place up. The wallpaper is about the drabbest you could imagine, but all Italian wallpaper seems to be the same. I took some photographs out of various magazines and mounted them on boards. I now want a huge vase of chrysanths on the central table. They seem quite plentiful here and would add a touch of colour.

There are no end of oranges about the district. There seem to be orange groves, or rather terraces, on every hillside.

Yesterday afternoon Jack and I walked down to a little tiny beach. There is a cliff some two or three hundred feet almost sheer above it and you get down from the road by a zig-zag path that goes most of the way through the rock. At the bottom the sand is dull grey, powdered rock presumably. There was a fair sized cave at one end that led through to an inlet in the sea or rather the entrance to another cave. The water was perfectly clear and just slightly tinged with blue. The rocks seem to have been affected by the sea, and were bright pink below the water level and green for eighteen inches or two feet above. It was one of those little glimpses of scenery that just take your breath away, the first time you see them.

The sea looked very calm and lovely and we promised ourselves a row this afternoon. But it rained all night and has been very wet this morning and so we shall have to postpone it. Italy is not by any means always sunny from our experience.

---

[*]To Sorrento.

We have had more rain in the couple of months we have been here, than we should have had in a year at home, as when it rains, it just tumbles down. One river rose nine feet in a few hours one day.

I wish you could have been with Jack and me when we went for a walk up the hillside. We kept getting the most marvellous views. As we looked out across the sea, we could see the silhouette of Capri, against the rays of the sun coming from behind a storm cloud, and the sea which the sun had turned silver. At one end of the island, there are some jagged teeth like the Needles and these looked particularly black in silhouette.

There was a great day some little time ago now, when the first train came along again. We were walking back when we heard the clanging of the bells and rattle on the line. All the Ities ran to their doors to see this wonder come along. I suppose it must have meant quite a lot in the return to normal life. In any case, they are an emotional and excitable race. When they talk English they are far too like the stage burlesque. One, the other day, was telling us that the Gerries had smashed the macaroni factory and with a flourish he said, "Anda nowa we hava no macarona." I hope they think our smiles are just friendliness.

(Of all the letters I wrote the only one to show any sign of censorship is the following. The words in brackets were obliterated, but not so successfully as to be unreadable.)

6. 12. 43.

We have had another very good day's outing, this time to (Capri). We crossed in quite a small boat, about thirty feet long I should think, and the sea was just choppy enough to add a spice of fun to the trip. I suppose the island is about three miles from the mainland, but it takes an hour and a half to get across. There was a pretty stiff wind and the current through the strait must be quite tricky.

(Capri) itself consists of two mountains, Tiberius and Augustus, with a sort of saddle between. The little town of (Capri) itself lies in the saddle, but the way up there is so steep that there is a funicular railway from the quay. The little harbour reminded me very much of the harbours in Cornwall, but the cliffs on either side are much higher of course.

We first went off to see the famous (Blue Grotto). This meant going in small rowing boats, manned by a couple of Ities, out from the harbour again and along rather more than half one side of the island. The entrance to the grotto is only just big enough to get a boat through; in fact, we had to change boats outside as ours from the harbour was just too big. The height of the hole is just about two feet six inches. We got flat in the bottom of the boat, while the boatman watched for the trough of the wave and we shot in. If he had gone in on the crest, he would have jammed himself up against the arch of the cave. I suppose it is because of this narrow entrance, that the grotto is so amazing. Imagine a cave about one hundred yards long and nowhere more than fifteen to twenty feet high, but with a dark roof and the water the most brilliant blue you have ever seen. It is just uncanny and like several other bits of nature I've seen, the Königsee at Berchtesgaden for example, it just took my breath away. The light is reflected through the water and produces this electric blue colour. No artificial means would ever produce anything like it.

Then we came back, had lunch, after going up to the town in the funicular, and then went on a car ride round the island. "Round" is a little wrong, as there are three roads, three prongs really, and one goes as far as one can along each and then comes back. The first prong we went along gave us some marvellous views of both Naples Bay and the Salerno Bay. The second prong led us down to (Gracie Fields' villa). This is on the south or Salerno side of the island. The house itself is about the tattiest you could imagine. It's just a one-storey dwelling. The furniture which we saw through the window certainly looked inviting though, with a grand piano in the lounge and a little green baby grand in the bedroom. Outside the lounge is a tessellated dance floor, on a terrace a couple of hundred feet above the sea, with an almost sheer drop to it. The grounds about are lovely though. They consist almost entirely of terraces from the house to the shore, but she has her own bathing beach there. She certainly knows a beautiful spot. The whole island is most delightful. I should like to go and explore again.

7. 12. 43.

I've had another day in Naples, really to hear a symphony concert by the San Carlo Opera House orchestra. It's rather amazing that this orchestra can give five concerts a week with the same programme mainly for the troops at about 1/- a time and make a profit.

It was worth going to see the opera house alone. I believe it is considered next best in Italy to La Scala at Milan. It is a typical continental opera house with plenty of crimson and gold about it, and with six tiers of boxes. There are just the stalls and then surrounding are these six tiers. The acoustics are perfect.

The concert was very good too. The orchestra excelled in the strings; woodwind and brass were not quite up to standard, but the Serenade of Tchaikovsky that they played for strings only was most delightful. The programme was fairly light, and included "The Dance of the Hours," also well played, and the Rackovsky March, but it also had in it Beethoven's Seventh Symphony. I particularly wanted to hear this and Jack "Die Fledermaus" - he is a Strauss fan. Unfortunately we must have lunched too well, or drunk too well, as he went to sleep during his bit and the slow movement of the symphony sent me off too.

There were a couple of singers too; the soprano was a real prima donna. They sang a duet from Butterfly and I should imagine it was just about as good as it could be.

We had lunch in the place I told you about before, down near the fishing quay. Once again there was the trio wandering round the tables and being most helpful in producing the right atmosphere. We had a couple of trios on Capri. One just consisted of two mandolins and played, among other stuff, "On the Isle of Capri". The wine we've been having lately has been Capri wine too, and very good and cheap, about 1/3 a bottle. The kind we have in our canteen by the way, is called Lacrimi Christi del Vesuvio or "Tears of the Christ of Vesuvius", a romantic name if ever there was one.

JACK

Jack comes into the story very frequently from Mareth onwards. He arrived as driver on our tank in somewhat of a storm metaphorically. Our crew of four had settled down quite well and, although a strange mixture, it worked, and more important still, lived together well. It is of the greatest importance that the crew should be well suited. It is not, of course, always possible to consider temperament when working out the battle order of a squadron, but other things being equal, I feel that the deciding question in the composition of a crew must be, "will they get on well together?" The four or five men live in such close proximity, that any obvious incompatibility must inevitably affect its working efficiency. In this particular case, the crew had been together a couple of months and had come to know each other. I suppose that if there were an odd man out, I was he, but I managed to keep enough contacts with the other three for this fact not to protrude too much.

Then quite suddenly one afternoon we were told that our driver was to go back with the echelon that evening, as another driver was coming up. He, we understood, was one of the original members of the regiment and had been out of things since Alamein. We did not like the idea and attempted to protest, but to no avail. And so Jack arrived.

He was not given a very warm welcome by the crew but, to his great credit, he realised what we felt. He settled into the crew quite quickly but, knowing him much better now, I am not surprised. This reconstituted crew went through the Mareth positions together, then on to Akarit. It was Jack who drove the tank through the minefields there on that nightmare ride. We went up to Sfax, making a triumphal entry into Sfax four hours or so after it had fallen. We were then separated from the unit and had become involved in a convoy moving through Sfax. We were the only tank and must have received acclamations that others far more deserved. It was our first experience of being "liberators" as distinct from "invaders". The people lined the road through the town and were almost delirious with their bravos and continual clapping. They gave us a good feeling that afternoon.

From there on we went up to the Enfidaville line, round to Medjez and eventually found ourselves in Tunis. It was in Tunis that Jack and I first drew very close to each other. There was day leave for us into Tunis after the fighting had finished, and Jack and I worked things so that we could go together. The first occasion was on a Sunday. We walked along the main boulevard there and quite curiously heard "Tipperary" coming from the windows of a fourth-storey room. We thought no more than to climb up to this room and just walk in. Before we had time to take anything in at all, we were seized, a cup put in our hands and that cup filled to the very brim. Having drunk to someone's health no doubt, we looked round the room and saw only a few British soldiers there, in spite of the noisy "Tipperary" reaching the street below. Most in the packed room were dressed in a dark bottle green battledress and wore berets. They were, we discovered, the conscript lads who had been in Tunisia at the fall of France and had been virtual prisoners there ever since. They were celebrating their freedom. Several of their fraternity had actually been imprisoned and one, released that afternoon, arrived while we were there. What hand-shaking and cheek-kissing there was for him! Meanwhile as they celebrated, they allowed our cups to be nothing but full to the brim.

I found this rather sweet, certainly delicious, Tunisian wine to be most good for my French too. I learnt the language for seven years at school but have always felt most self-conscious about using it. That, I believe, is the real reason that the British are not good linguists; we are too self-conscious. But two or three cups of Muscat is well calculated to break down anyone's self-consciousness. I found I was talking most fluent French, mostly to a family, the Abots, who lived in a flat on the same staircase. The gentleman was an optician from Bizerta, who had fled to Tunis on November 6th. 1942, when the Germans had arrived, only to be followed on November 11th. to Tunis. His wife had been lady's maid to the wife of a very prominent American and knew a few words of English, but she would not speak them. From this chance meeting we became friends, Jack and I visiting their flat on other occasions when we were in Tunis.

Later that afternoon we walked along the boulevard with the family. It was thronged with folk, all fraternising most healthily.

The promenade could not have held very many more, but everyone was happy, the French at the realisation that they were their own masters again, not realising all that this state of affairs involved, and the British that at least this long and sometimes discouraging campaign in Africa was finished; in their turn not realising that however important a step it was, it was but the first. As we walked from the boulevard to our car park, we found ourselves arm-in-arm with French lads of our own age. They were most friendly too. The whole city was pervaded in those early days by a sense of well-being.

This atmosphere could not, of course, last long. As the French attempted to resume a normal life and we were able to see the city in better perspective, it became obvious how much the Germans had looted from it. The shops were all empty. It did not matter what we asked for - and remember we had been in the desert then for four or five months, and needed small odds and ends - we were told "the Germans took them" - watch glasses, cotton and thread, and soap, to quote only three items. We heard tales of nationals being stopped on the road and their cars confiscated, they being left to complete their journey on foot, of flats being raided and carpets taken off the floors. We took these incidents as tales at that time, but our experience in Italy, afterwards, convinced us that they were probably true.

On leaving the city we had, on the first few visits, to go through the native quarters. Here the Arabs gave us as good a welcome as the French. They stood before their doors and clapped and cheered as we passed. I have a suspicion that the Arab is fickle, however. In Tripoli when Churchill had come to review us, I was standing across a side street, leading into the main road of the review. The Arabs were not allowed up that side street but crowded at the bottom. As Churchill drove by, we were most surprised to hear a round of applause coming from behind us. On the other hand, we were told everywhere, that the Arabs had got on very well with the Germans too - much better with the Germans than the Italians. And hence this reception in Tunis may not have been really genuine. In the state that the Arab world is in today, it may pay them to be friends with the top dog.

The wine that was procurable, mostly illicitly, in Tunis, went to the heads of the troops, and I saw more cases of drunkenness there than I have ever seen in the British Army. But the French population was most tolerant and instead of a puritanical frown, a smile would come across their faces when they saw a "drunk", and the words come from their lips "Il a bu"- which seems to me much more kindly than "He is drunk". The night of that first visit to Tunis, we returned with a couple of "corpses" on the floor of our truck, and Jack and I were happy too.

We returned from Tunis to a spot some seventy kilos east of Homs. The journey was made with our tanks on transporters and the whole six hundred and twenty miles took us five days. We saw a little more of Tunisia, Le Kef and Thola standing out in my mind particularly. From the approach to Le Kef, one would imagine a fine town, built on quite a prominent hill with its castle, presumably Moorish at the summit, but inside it was disappointing, just another squalid Arab settlement with few obviously European houses. When we passed through Thola, however, it was market day and looked most fascinating. The live stock seemed to be exclusively goats, although a few camels stood round the market square. The Arabs stood in their long robes, looking as if nothing in the world mattered and their transactions might take weeks to complete for all they cared.

We passed also through the Kasserine pass and the battlefield of February. There was still a number of knocked out tanks lying about the countryside, so completely out of place in that grand, open scenery. The pass looked to me almost impregnable. The gap in the range of hills could only be a few hundred yards wide, and the roadway through it was flanked on one side by an embankment and on the other side by mud-flats. And yet Rommel had pushed his Panzers into the mouth of the Pass. But whereas Alamein looked as if the Creator had intended it since the beginning of time to be a battlefield, Kasserine looked much more designed for peaceful pasture land and an idyllic country life.

It was on this journey too that we saw the full length of both the Akarit and Mareth defences. At Akarit the wadi had been hastily defended and yet the position looked most formidable. At Mareth, on the other hand, the Germans had retired to the old French fortifications, and the position looked to us from the top of a tank in a transporter, to be once again impregnable. How far along the road these defences ran, I do not know exactly, but it must have increased in number by two or three anti-tank ditches; every hillock, which commanded any view at all, had its pill-box dug into the top; minefields covered most of the rest of the area and were defended by barbed wire. And yet the Guards had penetrated three-quarters of these defences. It was without doubt Monty's brilliance in sending the left-hook round to El Hamma, that saved a heavy toll of life, for a frontal attack on such a position must have proved terrifically costly.

And so we passed on to Gafsas and Medinine and the Tunisian Tripolitanian border again. Medinine is one of the worst of all the Arab towns I have seen. It has the usual Moorish castle in the centre and round the hill are hovels built in tiers, four or five high. Each is a matter of a few square feet in area, with a semi-circular roof and housed a family. I believe I have read that the original Arabs at Medinine were troglodytic, and built their houses in this fashion to maintain the lay-out of caves. While we were fighting before Mareth, these Arabs had taken to the desert, but when we returned, their families were dwelling in these indescribable hovels once again.

The Tunisian border, Zuara, Tripoli and finally Homs, or to be exact, eight kilos east of Homs, was where we settled down to rest. The journey had been long but not tedious. We were seeing fresh scenes for the most part and when we were bored and tired of looking we read. Jack spent a fair part of the time in the turret and appeared at appropriate times with biscuits and cheese or jam. I sat on the front of the tank and went through three or four books in those five days. Strangely enough, I always read more when we were on the move, than when we were stationary. Reading was the great antidote to boredom and it was surprising where all the books came from. I had a parcel from home quite frequently and however much appreciated the other contents were, the books were always the most welcome. We did not have to read any "throw-outs" from old spinsters' libraries either, which I feared we might be reduced to before we left. I read "The Keys of the Kingdom", "Black-out in Gretley" and "The last train from Berlin" within a few months of their publication, for example. On this journey down from Tunis, I remember I read and enjoyed thoroughly, Sacheverell Sitwell's "Before the Bombardment". It was a Penguin edition and even if these six-penny paper-backed novels had not justified their existence before the war, which I doubt, they have more than done so since. The backbone of an army library in North Africa was always a row of Penguins and the similar publications.

At Homs we found ourselves encamped in a date grove. We pitched our bivvies in neat little rows between the trees and our troops were only some fifty yards from wog dwellings. Watching the cultivation of these primitive folk was one of our main occupations, during our stay there. When we arrived, the date-palms were just in blossom, although we did not realise it until, sitting under one, we would feel something small and hard hit our heads. It would be the flower, a very small, white, four-petalled and waxy blossom. Before we left, the dates had formed and filled out almost to their full size, although they were still very green.

Then, soon after we arrived, these wogs ploughed the sand, or to be perfectly truthful, they watched their women folk plough. Frequently we saw the women working, ploughing, reaping, threshing, while the man of the house had curled himself up in his blanket underneath a palm. The plough was nothing more really than a wedge of wood and was pulled through the sand by a camel or a cow, to the accompaniment of much heaving and many weird noises from the woman driver.

The sand was then watered from a well. It was one of the pulley variety; here all wells seemed to be of the same kind. We first knew of its existence about four-thirty one morning when its screeching woke us up and kept us awake. I think the noise must have some superstitious significance for the Arabs, as some of our fellows greased a wheel with car grease one morning after a similar experience, and the Arabs immediately packed up and went. The goatskin was pulled up by a cow, always a cow, which went methodically, hour after hour, up and down a ramp which the wog had dug. These wells, with their bold overhead structure, pulley and sloping ramp, were a feature of Tripolitania.

The water was raised into a stone trough and the flow controlled from there. Small channels, some six inches wide, led down from the trough to the tilled ground and were dammed at appropriate places, in order to direct the water where it was wanted. The actual cultivated area was divided into small squares by sand walls and the water allowed into two or three of these squares at a time.

These squares were then sowed with the seed of, I presume, Indian corn, although later the ear seemed very small and indifferent. A very few days later the first blade showed through and in ten days or a fortnight it was six inches high. The wog then thinned out, the surplus being given to the camels that placidly stood by and watched the proceedings. Then it seemed there was nothing to be done for several weeks apart from occasional watering and bird scaring. I have read of this occupation in parts of rural England, but I have never seen or heard it myself. In Tripolitania, the wog would walk round banging tins, possibly one of our bully tins salvaged from the waste pit, and crying out most weirdly for the whole of the daylight. We did not appreciate these efforts.

I suppose it was no more than four weeks later that this corn was six to eight feet high. It remained at this stage, for a few days ripening and was then cut, by a hand sickle. The women took great armfuls and plucked the ears from the straw. The ears were then thrown on the ground and trampled on by any available animal. The camel, the donkey, the cow and the next door neighbour's cow were tied together, the inside animal facing the opposite way and driven round and round over the ears. The smallest child took its part in chasing the poor, unfortunate animals round. It took several days to thresh the crop in this way. The result was put into a straw basket and sifted out from shoulder height, the principle being, I take it, that the chaff would drift away in the breeze and the heavier corn fall to the ground. Once again this winnowing took several days. With the storing of the corn in sacks, the process ended.

It took about nine weeks for the whole of this work to be completed, from the original ploughing to the storing of the corn. We were not at the spot long enough to see whether there was time for a second crop to be grown that season, although since the first crop had been dealt with by early August, I should imagine that there would be ample time.

As I said before, watching these wogs at close quarters provided us with one of our main entertainments during this summer. Once a week the man of the house used to take the camel and donkey with him off to market in Homs. He seldom returned with much merchandise. When it grew hotter, a tent was pitched outside the stone house and the men slept there.

This tent was also used to entertain the guests when there was a wedding in the family. The tent was enlarged the night before and early in the morning all the male Arabs appeared in their cleanest clothes. Quite soon the musicians arrived, beating drums and playing bagpipes as they approached the house. The women welcomed them from the roof with a high-pitched warbling note, rather like the film version of the Red Indian call. These musicians then took up their positions in the tent and the guests began to arrive. A number of us went across and were interested in the festivities. We found the bagpipes consisted of a sack affixed to a representation of a bull's head, with horns and eyes. From the mouth came the reed pipe. This pipe had only four holes and consequently, the range and variety of the melodies were somewhat limited. The drummer was really in charge, however. It was he who worked on the feelings of the company.

I remember lying in bed one night and hearing one of these drums in the distance. I was too far away to hear the pipes. The drum would beat some complex rhythm quite quietly and slowly. It gathered speed and vigour until five minutes later it infused even me, with an enthusiasm that was obviously felt more keenly in the assembled company, for there they had become noisy and excited. The drummer at this wedding would do the same.

We also bought an invitation to the wedding. Each guest, on arriving, produces a coin, or in these days a bank-note, spits on it and, as the pipes are playing, sticks it on the piper's forehead. We put the Allied Military commission notes on his head and were presumably guests from that moment. It seems to me quite a good scheme, for the bride's father to get the wedding expenses in this way.

Unfortunately the actual wedding ceremony I missed. I had a temperature that night, a little incipient malaria, and had to go to bed. I saw the next day the bride go off to her future house. On a very fine Arab horse was a saddle enclosed in curtains. The bridegroom led the horse and the male guests followed, wailing most horribly, exactly as if at a funeral. This little procession trailed over the sand hills to a native village a mile or so away. A number of sheep turned up at the father's and I wondered many times when I saw them if they were the price of the bride.

We were rather far from entertainment and civilisation in this camp and for the most part had to find our own amusements. Bathing, naturally, provided a daily sport. It was as good as I have found anywhere. The beach shelved very slowly down and was completely sandy. The water was usually just warm enough not to give us a rude shock, and yet not so warm that the bathe was not refreshing. Moreover, we did not have to worry about the tide. There is a tide in the Mediterranean, in spite of what geography text books say, but it is so slight that it does not affect bathing. On this beach there seemed to be a difference of four or five feet up the beach between high and low tide, and of four to six inches in level.

Jack came into his own in the water. He was a great seal, thrashing his way through, or diving to the bottom. Not very much serious swimming was done, although one of our Squadron covered himself with oil one Sunday morning and swam from Homs to the camp, some eight miles. Most were happy enough to splash about and enjoy themselves fooling with each other. Quite a number learnt to swim, a feat which was supposed to be good training for future operations!

In the afternoons we usually played bridge. I believe it is contrary to King's Regulations for Other Ranks to play bridge, but after one has learnt the game, no other is satisfying. I improved my game beyond measure during these weeks. But eventually it was too hot even to play cards. There were a number of dust storms during this period. I have said something about them before. They are called "Khamsin", from the Arabic for fifty, I am told, as legend says that fifty thousand devils ride to produce this cloud of dust. It was an old Arabic law, too, that if a dust storm persisted for five days, murder was excusable. I can understand that ruling and sympathise with it. Usually a storm would last for three days and even then tempers became frayed. Dust driving into bivvies, hair, food, eyes, clothing, everywhere, will irritate even the most patient. And three days of irritation is usually sufficient to finish off the normal temper. On two occasions this year we had dust storms lasting for five days and believe me, anything would have been excusable then.

Although it seems intensely hot in one of these Khamsins and it is difficult to breathe, it was actually hotter a fortnight or so after the last dust storm. That day in Tunis when we had met the Abots, Madame was wearing a little brooch arrangement. I asked her what it was and she took it off to show me. It was a thermometer and she pinned it on my shirt "pour un souvenir". I used this thermometer to register the heat during these afternoons. I do not know off-hand the correct formula for changing centigrade to Fahrenheit. My little thermometer frequently registered 46 deg. and I make that out to be approaching 120 deg. in the shade!

If we sat under a tree to benefit from what little breeze there was, we had to move round with the sun. If we sat under a tent, it became a hothouse. The best and coolest place was the beach and finally we rigged up there a cover of an old Italian ground sheet and spent the afternoon under it.

We had a little stage built on the beach and three or four shows were given there. They were the usual army vaudeville performances on the whole. I think it is a pity that the old Concert Party has died out - half-a-dozen or eight artistes who put together a show between them. Such a performance would call for more versatility than the usual amateur seems to have today. As it is, every army show consists of the same items; the crooner, the piano accordionist, the funny man, with perhaps a vamp pianist or a mouth-organ thrown in.

A few of us attempted to do a show of rather a different style. We wrote the script and produced a skit on the average soldier's idea of a cavalry regiment, with all its spit and polish and old school tie. When we gave this sketch to our own unit, it was possible to get any number of cracks at individuals, from the Colonel downwards, and it could not fail. It also went down very well when we did it outside. We were willing to carry on and form ourselves into a regular Concert Party, but there was so little help from the powers that be, that it was impossible. We had no guarantee that fellows would be released from fatigues for rehearsals, for example. And any chap who is willing to give up the hours to rehearsal, that even the least ambitious show demands, deserves to get off a fatigue or two.

In Homs itself, there were two places of entertainment, a cinema and a theatre. Since both seated only two hundred and fifty and there were some thousands to be catered for, these were hardly adequate. The great saving factor was the Roman theatre at Leptis Magna. Two kilos east of Homs are the ruins of this one-time important Roman port. In some ways, they are more perfect and more interesting than those at Pompeii. The houses, the baths, the little narrow streets, the wide open forum, all stand to be seen these centuries later, and the theatre served five thousand troops nightly, of a vastly different character from the legionaries that have marched along the North African coast.

There was still much evidence of restoration in this theatre. Behind the stage were three columns ready to be hoisted beside their standing brothers. In the orchestra were the capitols for these columns and on either side of the amphitheatre were great structures of scaffolding. But even as it was, it provided seats for five thousand. A small platform was built in front of the orchestra and sacking, suspiciously like target canvas, was drawn from end to end behind it. There was, there could be, no front curtain, and the players were curiously near and intimate with their vast audience.

I saw several good shows here. They were provided by Ensa or neighbouring Army Units. The best of these that I saw was the Concert Party from the Seventh Convalescent Depot. It had a good compere, who could put over the modern ballad song, "I was her man but she done me wrong" type, as well as I have heard. It had a drummer in its band, a good one too, who could clown. And on this particular occasion, it had a drill sergeant from the Guards (presumably) who gave the audience a brilliant army instructional lecture on the table knife.

The high spot of the Ensa shows was an all-star evening with Leslie Henson, Beatrice Lillie, Dorothy Dickson and Vivien Leigh. Leslie Henson made a mock speech and cracked a gag which must succeed in that audience.

"I was told years ago that if I did not give up drinking, I should see before me thousands and thousands of rats and now (with a shrug of his shoulders) it's come true."

Beatrice Lillie is always a joy to hear and even though I was perched right at the back of this huge auditorium and was standing on one leg for most of the show, I enjoyed every word of all her songs. The pathos of "Wind round my heart" I shall never forget.

During these three or four months, the only leave arrangements we could make were to go into Tripoli for a day or four days. If we went for one day, we left early one morning, arrived in Tripoli about midday, left again about eight o'clock, went ten or twelve miles outside, bedded down for the night and finished the journey the next day. The four-day leave period was spent in a Rest Camp where there were so many that we queued for one and a half to two hours for every meal. I only went on day leaves as I could not face a "rest" under such conditions.

Jack and I spent one very pleasant day on such a leave there. We had a gharry and drove along the front. We went to a film; a Sonja Henie affair, the title of which I have forgotten, and generally had a pleasant time doing nothing in particular. By this time, entertainments had been more strongly organised. The Balbo Soldier's Home had become the "Union Club" and had a cinema, a bazaar, a Naafi, a rest room, a writing room and so on. The Y.M.C.A. had opened there.

The Miramere Theatre was being used, although on this occasion I was bitten by fleas or bugs - for only the second time between leaving England and arriving back. Cafés were open for the sale of soft drinks and cakes. Tripoli was a much pleasanter, although by no means hectic, place.

Eventually it was time for us to do a little move towards winning this war. We were fully equipped again and wondered what our role would be. When Italy fell and it was announced that the American Fifth Army had landed at Salerno, we knew.

Jack had by this time changed his job. He had gone to the Reconnaissance Squadron and hence on operations, I should not see nearly as much of him. When we concentrated at Tripoli, before going over, we managed to spend another afternoon in the town and only regretted that it was not at Tunis where we could celebrate properly.

We loaded up in tank-landing ships and started off. These craft are quite amazing for the speed with which they can be both loaded and unloaded. I believe they will revolutionise coastwise shipping after the war. Our ship was manned by American coast guards and a very pleasant bunch of fellows they seemed. Our tank crew got to know two of them very well in the few days that we were on board. We had a can of Tunisian wine with us and they lapped it up, although to our palate it was poison. We entertained them each night and swapped yarns. They were both childishly anxious to acquire some Gerry souvenirs. By this time, four months after Tunis, we had disposed of most of our "loot", but I had a German infantry belt right at the bottom of my valise and one of these Yanks was terrifically excited with it. I wish I could have given him more.

The crossing passed most pleasantly. The sea was calm and still, and the route interesting, and I was quite sorry, for this reason alone apart from more obvious ones, when we eventually arrived in Salerno Bay. The bridgehead was fairly well established then, the sticky days had passed, and Salerno was in our hands, but the hills on the north of the bay, in the Sorrento Peninsula, were still in Gerry hands and there were apparently still some guns in those hills, probably in the monastery at the top, with a German observation officer fuming madly when so many good targets were blotted out.

Unfortunately we kept the Navy and its smoke pretty busy that day. There was a sand bank some hundred yards from the shore and our boat would not ride it. We made a dash but were stuck. We hauled back on the anchor chain, made another dash and were still stuck. We did this four times. Then some of the equipment we were carrying was taken off in the middle of the bay, in a smaller landing craft. We had a fifth attempt and still failed. More trucks had to come off and at last, at ten o'clock at night, in the sixth attempt, our boat reached the beach. We had spent ten hours in these six attempts; and yet during all that time there had been only about four shells and the nearest was some two hundred yards off. There was, at this time too, a great quantity of shipping in the bay, but nothing was hit that day.

Several times during the campaign, I found myself surprised that the scene looked so much as it ought to look! The chaos behind the battlefield at Alamein had looked as if it were a representation in a Hollywood studio, and here at Salerno, the beach looked as if it were a painted canvas by a war artist. There were wire-matting runways for the tank from the larger landing craft to the road above the beach. There were odd lorries pitched here and there. There were dumps of petrol. There were amphibious jeeps, so rightly called "ducks," running about on the beach and taking to the water just like their namesakes. There was the isolated A.A. gun - with its small crew sitting round its entrenchment. There were a hundred and one small details which seemed to exaggerate the reality of the scene.

We soon found when we landed that Italy was the land of fruit. Our first leaguer was in an orchard. Along one side ran the largest plantation of tomatoes I have ever seen, acres and acres of them. These were of the queer plum-shaped variety, but very tasty, and we had tomatoes for every meal for several days. In the orchard itself were apples and walnut trees and oranges and lemons. Unfortunately, none of these were ripe. We ate greedily for the first few days and then settled down to a regular diet for the remainder of our stay in Italy.

The farmhouse in the centre of the orchard had been used as a German Headquarters and had been shelled by our naval guns in the first few days of the landing. One poor old man had had his leg shattered and was still in the granary when we arrived.

The peasantry were both suspicious and superstitious. They at first refused the help of our medical officers, but that night there was some sort of religious service going on in the granary. It was uncanny to stand listening in the twilight to the plain-song chanting, led by a woman. The next day, however, better counsels prevailed, and the old man was removed in our ambulance. Although gangrenous, his leg had a good chance of recovery. This case was the first of a civilian casualty which we had come across, and brought home to us very forcibly the horror and futility of war.

As soon as we got on the move, we also found that Italy was the land of rain and the railway posters of "Sunny Italy" may be true of some parts of the year and some parts of the country, but the Naples plain in September 1943 was much more a "Rainy Italy". As we were standing in our column at mid-afternoon in Salerno itself, a wind sprang up and within a minute the rain was lashing down. But this storm was merely a foretaste of what was to come. That night we pulled up just through the hills of Salerno at last light. Almost immediately a hurricane or tornado or something arose. Tank sheets were ripped off and carried down the street. Some bed-rolls were even lifted off the tanks. Then came a deluge. It was rain such as I had never seen before. Two minutes after it had started, water several inches deep was rushing down the street. Those fellows who had already unrolled their beds, found them swamped. The remainder of the bed-rolls, not still in the tanks, were standing in water. I myself had decided to sleep in the turret that night and was the only one of the crew with anything like dry blankets for several days. A true baptism into Italian warfare!

The weather was never settled during all the time we were in Italy. For hours there would be a typical blue Italian sky and then it would cloud over and rain begin. It was cold at night too. But we had been warned of such conditions. Whatever the travelogues on Italy said before the war, the army authorities had told us that we were going to a land of rain.

The third feature of Italy in September that we soon discovered was the mosquitoes. We had, of course, met them in North Africa. I had, in fact, been bitten by a malaria-carrying lady and spent a very recent month in hospital. But in Italy they were numerous enough to be a pest. At twilight they began their aerial attack and would zoom round our heads, looking for a good run-in before they finally dive-bombed our foreheads or necks. We learnt immediately to use the anti-mosquito cream, the new variety of which was most effective in keeping off this plague. Head nets came out too, and were draped over our foreheads and necks although they were rarely pulled down over our faces, as it was both difficult to see and breathe with the netting over our eyes and noses. I do not think that the type of mosquito we met in the first days in Italy was malaria-carrying, however.

The fighting in Italy was, of course, vastly different from that we had grown used to in North Africa. There was no chance of deployment or quick manoeuvre but, I fancy, our Command learnt many lessons in close-country warfare in the first two days of action in Italy.

The route from Salerno to Volturno, the ultimate objective of the first series of leaps, lay to the north-east of Vesuvius, skirting the northerly Naples suburbs, through San Marcellino and Albanova to San Maria la Fossa and eventually Grazzanisse.

I did a guard under Vesuvius although never had I, in the wildest flights of imagination, thought I would ever study a volcano under such circumstances. He was then puffing red-hot cinders out of his bowl every ten seconds. There was a brilliant shower of sparks which appeared to fall quite slowly, and to have hardly died away, when the next shower would shoot up. During the daytime, he was apparently puffing out a good stream of smoke which drifted far away into the distance. Later, when we visited Vesuvius, the watchers told us that they were expecting a major eruption at any time. Actually, it was three months before the lava stream obliterated San Sebastiano, threatening Torre Annunziata, and forced troops thirty miles away in Salerno to wear steel helmets.

The worst sight of this advance was at Guigliano, where a German multiple mortar had shelled a crossroads in the middle of the village. It was quite easy to see where the six rounds had fallen or hit and why so many Americans had been caught.

But the unforgettable experience was to witness for ourselves the results of, or to hear about, the German atrocities. Previously we had all been a little sceptical of atrocity stories; I certainly had myself, and regarded them as so much propaganda, that is half truth and half fabrication. But now I know that no atrocity story could possibly exaggerate the lengths to which this enemy of ours will go.

We had heard tales from several villagers of what was going on further up. But our first actual experience of this kind was when our column of tanks was in a very narrow lane. There was hardly room for a pedestrian to pass on either side. Coming against the column, however, was a funeral procession, coffin carried in front and followed by priest and mourners. For some reason the priest stopped at our tank and asked us if any of us spoke Italian. He was a typical country parish priest, a little pathetic in his torn lace surplice and faded blue stole. We said we did not know much Italian, but asked him to carry on as we might be able to understand. And with the help of gestures, he told us that he was burying a girl of seventeen who had been murdered and raped the previous afternoon. A group of girls, all weeping, went by on the other side of the tank and the priest told us that they too had been raped.

The next morning we passed the body of a girl lying in the field about fifty yards from the road. She too had suffered a like fate. Since these girls were presumably murdered because they had resisted, they must have been murdered and raped in that order.

Again, we passed through Parete the same night just before dark. Some fifty trees had been blasted down on either side of the road and fallen across the road. The obstacle took some time to circumvent and it was late in the afternoon when we moved again. In the dusk, therefore, against the wall of the church of Parete, we could see some eleven corpses. One was that of an old man in his night-shirt. The tale that we were told by the villagers was that a German soldier had been attacked and that as a reprisal a certain number of men, varying between twelve and eighteen, had been rounded up summarily and shot. An armed guard had been mounted over their bodies and no relatives allowed near, although the murders had taken place four days before we arrived. Then, already the relatives were taking away the corpses in coffins, although the Germans had only left half an hour before.

Perhaps the most poignant example of this barbarism we met was just outside Albanova. We drew up in an orchard where, incidentally, there were the most delicious apples I have ever tasted. In the farm building was a typical Italian family, rather obviously scared when we first arrived. When we came to know the father better and had, to some extent, won his confidence, he told us that a couple of Nazi youths, aged about seventeen, had come into his house one day, placed the forearms of his three year old son on the table, and chopped off his hands with a bayonet. We verified this story as much as we could, that is, to the extent of seeing the child with the two stumps wrapped in filthy bandages.

The fighting in Italy was not very severe as far as we were involved. Only today, as I write sitting in a Norman orchard, I have read in the newspaper that the division encountered and beat in Italy the fifteenth Panzer Division, but our small part of the division met few of its tanks. The only occasion on which I remember we suffered from tanks was at the village of Arzano. The regimental column had approached the village square and the leading recce and tank troops were beyond it, with regimental headquarters in the centre of the town. Recce reported a pylon felled across the road and on examination found that the area round it was mined, while the pylon itself was booby-trapped. Our recce boys cleared sufficient mines to make a diversion round the pylon and a troop was deployed and went up. Then things happened with the result that three tanks were lost and four lives. It was thought afterwards that at least one anti-tank gun and one tank or possibly two tanks or guns were hidden in the foliage, covering this obstacle from about one hundred and fifty yards.

While this miniature battle was going on in front of the village, a report came through that infantry were infiltrating on our flanks. We therefore placed our tanks across all entries to the main road. It was a most uncomfortable time, as I felt continually that the infantry might quite well have come along the flat Italian roofs and caused quite a disturbance, dropping things from the tops. However, none of us actually saw any of these infantry. That night was most uncomfortable too. We were packed into the square and adjoining streets of the town and all Italians were told to be in their houses by six o'clock. After that hour, our orders were to shoot at sight anyone moving about street level. The whole night long it felt uncannily as if someone were moving about the village. But the next morning things had quietened down again and we carried on to Albanova.

The obstacles of the fallen trees, which I have mentioned before, kept us waiting here some hours and when we eventually reached our objective it was nightfall. The final 24 miles seemed more like ten and we fetched up about 8 o'clock with a host of twinkling lights before us. These naturally aroused the suspicion of our leading reconnaissance officer and he and a sergeant did a foot recce, attacking the lights from the left, to see what they were all about. They proved to be oil lamps waved by forty Italians, partly in greeting, partly as a warning that the Germans had laid mines on the surface of the roads. The local policeman volunteered to collect a band and lift these mines in the morning, which they actually did.

We got to know Albanova pretty well before we left Italy as we spent some three or four weeks there after coming out of action. It was a dirty, squalid village of some fair size. The streets were cobbled and almost perpetually covered with dung and vegetable refuse. The houses looked little cleaner. All these houses seemed to be constructed in the usual Italian manner - fronted straight on to the street, but built inside around a courtyard with a balcony running around the first floor. Inside the courtyard, things looked brighter, as there were frequently flowers.

The one family we got to know in this village reminded us of the Marx brothers. We went to them first as tailors, to get a new issue of greatcoats altered. There were three brothers, all deaf and dumb, a sister who did all the talking and made up for her brothers, and the parents, the old man in his cloak and broad-brimmed hat resembling a Martini advertisement. Two of the brothers were tailors, the third a cobbler, and all turned out remarkable work. But as they were shock headed, the curly type of Italian, and gesticulated violently in order to express themselves, they looked like three comedians from the silent film days.

The only other battle experience we had in Italy was the crossing of the Volturno. This river is a rapid, muddy stream with steep banks and about 90 feet across in our sector of the line. We approached the river and our supporting infantry - or did the tanks in Italy support the infantry? - sat and watched for several days. Patrols were sent across at night either in boats or swimming and Jerry patrols returned the visits. It was usually necessary to get a line across by the first fellow as the downstream movement in such a current was frequently as much as 70 yards and the boats had to haul along the line to keep anything like a straight course.

Eventually a company established itself on the other side and this little footing was enlarged to a bridgehead. A Bailey bridge was put across in very quick time but it was not heavy enough for tanks and the only other bridge at that time across, at Capua, was already sufficiently committed. Our tanks must therefore be waterproofed and taken through the water. We went back to Naples to have the necessary modifications put on the tanks and we were ready in 48 hours. Incidentally, waterproofing for the second front took more than a week.

The colonel himself had sounded the river for a crossing which proved to be alongside the bridge. Some of our fellows became engineers, or pioneers, and dug though the steep banks to prepare a ramp down for the tanks. As this way down came from the road leading to the bridge, there was a nasty right-handed turn immediately on entering the water.

After some days, perhaps a fortnight, on the north bank of the Volturno, we were withdrawn, first to Albanova and then to Sorrento, and later informed that we were coming home. The period, some six to eight weeks, between coming out of action and getting onto the boat, were a very pleasant "holiday" in a delightful part of Italy.

We visited Naples, Pompeii and Capri and generally made the most of the opportunities.

At first, Naples was a rather a war-scarred city. Near the docks and the harbours, our air forces had caused a considerable amount of damage, but a hundred yards back and in the remainder of the city, the only evidence of the battle experience was damage caused by blast. In the early days, the city was rather dead; shops were mainly closed and the restaurants not open either.

However, quite quickly really, life returned to something like normal. The Via Roma was packed with troops and civilians. The crowd reminded me of the Saturday afternoon mass in a market town. The shops were not badly stocked but most of their merchandise was expensive. Restaurants opened, supplied, I suspect, largely from the black market, and the inevitable musicians appeared.

Jack and I found a delightful place to eat - the Bersiglieri on the fishing quay. It was large with glass partitions overlooking the little harbour. The food was good and the wine excellent. I think it was here that we first sampled Capri wine. I remember on our first visit there was roast tunny on the menu too. And macaroni, which must have been bought on the black market.

Later, at Sorrento, we were told that the Germans had packed as much explosive into the macaroni factory at Castellamare as possible and then blown it up, and our informant concluded with an appropriate gesture of his hands, "and now we hava no macarone," which was a serious thing for the poor Italians!

At Sorrento, on the southern side of the Naples Bay, it was in a most delightful district, high precipitous mountains rising from the road at their feet and orange groves covering the towering slopes. There were still plenty of oranges on the trees but as it was November the fruit needed protection from the frosts which were just then beginning. Lattice panels, resting on large scaffoldings, therefore covered the groves.

We had a daily supply of oranges, tangerines and mandarins. I looked after a reading room for my squadron and each morning I collected up the cigarette ends for an old man who gave me a morning call. Each morning he came but I never heard him speak a word. By signs he would tell me that his rheumatics were bad, then produce three or four oranges or tangerines, whereupon I would present him with the dog-ends. He was duly overjoyed, shook hands several times and, almost weeping, tottered out.

One afternoon Jack and I climbed up the steep path of the mountain to cross over to the Salerno side of the promontory at St. Agatha. A couple of lads road sweeping asked us for a cigarette with which we obliged them and very promptly disappeared into an orchard, bringing back oranges in return.

It was on that walk that we had the most marvellous view of Capri. The sky became stormy, and a dark sullen cloud stretched across from horizon to horizon; but underneath, the sun blazed with the piercing golden light of a stormy afternoon. Against the brilliance, Capri, with its sharp mountainous outline, stood silhouetted.

The boats are quite small, holding sixty passengers at the most. We took up places in the bows and watched the coastline of the mainland, as we hugged it round until we reached the narrowest part of the crossing. Then the boat turned straight to Capri. There is naturally quite a swell forcing its way through the gap, and the little boat rode each wave as it came to it. For those who could stand the sudden drops into the trough of the wave, it was a grand sensation, but I remember one at least of the party, who soon took on a hue of deep pea green. Spray added to the fortunes of the crossing and we were all slightly wet, when eventually we reached the lee of the island and tied up in the harbour of Marina Majora.

Here we found dozens of small white boats, almost like the Rob-roys and pleasure boats on the children's boating pond or the seaside lake. They were the transport for the Blue Grotto and as there is only one Blue Grotto in the world, we decided that our first visit on the island must be there.

We followed the coast along for some considerable way, tossing slightly in the little coracle until we eventually came to a small hole in the cliff. I suppose the hole was about three feet wide and two feet six inches high. Anyhow, it was too small for our boat to go through and we had to transfer to another of smaller width. We approached the hole and the boatman told us to lie flat in the boat. He, himself, caught hold of a chain going through the hole, judged the trough of a wave, pulled hard, subsided to the bottom of the boat also, and we shot into the Blue Grotto.

What I saw took my breath away. I have experienced this sensation before, walking over the top of the Pennines and suddenly coming upon Ewden Glen or hearing the echo of the bugle from the cliff face on the Königsee. The Blue Grotto achieved this phenomenon every bit as much. Coming out of the sunlight, the first vision was one of intense black above and intense blue below, a topsy turvy scene. When our eyes grew accustomed to the light, we could make out the roof of this cave, perhaps thirty or forty feet high and a hundred yards or so in depth, but the water never lost its brilliant blueness. Looking down over the boat it was pale blue, which shaded in depths of ultra-marine at the side of the cave. A most marvellous experience, yet one which I do not want to repeat. Neither Ewden Glen nor the Königsee were as good on a second visit, and I want the Blue Grotto to retain in my memory the wonder of this first visit.

On our return to the harbour, we went by a funicular railway up to the town of Capri itself. It is a quaint town of narrow streets and small shops, all obviously catering for the tourist. We found a hotel for lunch and once again fed well and wined well, with Capri wine in its true setting. The vegetable soup though, seemed to consist of one cauliflower each.

After lunch we hired an open touring car and went "round the island". This trip consists really of going as far as one can along the road, to Anna Capri; then retracing one's path and going as far as possible in the other direction, to Marina Minora, on the Salerno side of the island. Both roads climb uphill and descend in the reverse direction and present one continually with magnificent seascapes. The climb to Anna Capri gave us one of the most magnificent views of the Naples Bay and Vesuvius that we had seen.

The whole of the bay is always dominated by Vesuvius. There he is all the time with the cloud of smoke drifting away from his cone. There are mountains all round the bay and Ischia in the north, and Capri in the south are mountainous islands, but the azure blue of the bay is always commanded by Vesuvius and one's eye always eventually finds its way to the volcano.

Returning from Anna Capri, Mussolini's villa built on the top of the opposite mountain, seemed to suggest his aloofness from the common herd. The second famous villa we visited was Gracie Fields's. It is at Marina Minora and the terraces and beach are really in the Salerno Bay. The grounds are charming and the terrace, used, we were told, for dancing and built outside the villa, suggested sweet music and the soft lights of a Mediterranean night sky. But the villa was most disappointing. It was a one-storey Italian house and hardly lived up to the imposing name of villa.

But Capri is a lovely place. I suppose some would scorn it as too popular; but after all, the populace drifts towards places that are worthwhile. Garmisch may be spoilt by the number of winter sportsmen and women that go there but it still is a lovely place and so is Capri. We were actually billeted in San Angelo which was a contiguous little township to Sorrento, and again on the other side joined Piano di Sorrento. We lived in the municipal school which also housed some of the municipal offices. For example, there was a weekly queue which began to form in the early hours of the morning and chattered its time away below our window until the food office opened at 10 o'clock. It was for the weekly food tickets. The Italians had a queer idea of queuing in that the men and women formed separate queues on either side of the door.

I was quite impressed by the school. It was an oldish building of about the time of most of the London schools, that is pre-the-last war. But its decoration was comparatively modern and its rooms were light, clean and airily enamelled in royal blue and white. The furniture, on the other hand, belonged to the original period and could not be compared to modern English school furniture.

On the street level there had been some shops, but these, with the exception of the food office, were either closed or used by us for regimental purposes. One was the orderly room, another the chapel and a third the reading room I have mentioned before. This reading room proved a great boon. I, myself, played bridge in it almost every night and it was always used well for cards, reading or writing. Since I was in sole charge, I tried one or two ideas I have always believed to be sound principles. I wanted the fellows to respect the room and its furniture. There was therefore a notice at the door, "You will remove your hat, won't you?" Moreover, I felt that the fellows would respect it more if the custodian obviously respected it and the floor was consequently washed every morning - the only room in the building to receive that attention - the windows were clean, a few, three to be precise, pictures manufactured for the walls, and flowers procured for the table. As those in bloom at the time were either carnations or the showy chrysanthemums, there was always a good display on the table. Round the corner was the regimental canteen which, to my mind, never acquired quite the same atmosphere. It provided Jack and me though with wine and so quite adequately fulfilled its purpose. Most of the wine we got here went by the name of "Lacrimae Christi del Vesuvio", "Tears of the Christ of Vesuvius". It was a good wine, for those who like the dry Italian wines, but I think nothing quite approached that Caprian vintage we drank on our first visit to the Bersiglieri.

At Piano there was a cinema, a horrible little place really, but it provided us with entertainment of a kind, and I can still remember some of the films I saw there, which says much for its usefulness. "I married a Witch", was as good a light comedy as I had seen on the screen but as far as I can find out has not yet, almost a year later, appeared on the English screen. "The Gold Rush" shows the passage of time badly. Perhaps because it had an Italian commentary, it failed badly. Charlie Chaplin's earlier films do not rehash very well. On the other hand, I saw "Pride and Prejudice," there for the third time and could have seen it willingly three more times that week.

There was a cinema also at Sorrento, but the current surged and spoilt the sound. Propaganda, I suppose it was, dictated that we should give the Italians as much opera as possible and therefore Deanna Durbin films came frequently, but at Sorrento the apparatus did little justice to her voice.

There is a glamour for us about this stay on the south of the Naples Bay but why should there not be? We had come out of action, we were going home and we were staying in part of the world where American wealthies spent their millions to sojourn in the winter.

Eventually we moved from Sorrento and stayed in a transit - or transitory camp - for one night at Casoria before finally embarking. We left in the very early hours of the morning to march the seven or eight miles to the docks. We all dreaded this march in battle order but really understood that it was worthwhile. It did not seem too long, however, and was enlivened by a bagpipe accompaniment from the M.O.

He was a Scotsman and produced his bagpipes at most unusual times. It was almost a regular feature for him to practise for an hour or so after arriving in leaguer and I well remember him marching round the sand dunes of Mareth in the rain shortly after he had joined the regiment. Then again there was that occasion before the Volturno when he strutted in slow march, playing the "Skye Boat Song" from the echelon where he lived, to where our three tanks were parked, a matter of five or six hundred yards, with the Italian peasantry wondering what on earth it was all about. But his "music" on the way to the docks at Naples cheered a rather dreary march enormously and probably woke up many unoffending Ities in the very small hours of the morning.

The march itself went fairly quickly but there was an interminable shuffle though Naples itself and onto the boat. A wait of half an hour enabled us to have breakfast on the kerb stone but mostly it was a move of a few hundred yards and then a stop. Our regiment was the last but one to embark and hence the delay. How many were eventually packed on to the boat, heaven knows. I doubt even if heaven did. It was considerably more than it had ever held before, though. The arrangements were almost identical to those in the boat going out. The decks were filled to capacity and then some more. The tables to seat 18, held 22 because of the extra numbers. The hammocks touched each other fore and aft and on both sides. The tables and decks were covered with bodies for which there were no hammocks.

In the first part of the morning these main decks had to be cleared and inspected. Then everyone but orderlies must be above decks and at 9.30 there was a muster parade at boat stations. It was therefore quite impossible, which meant only that one could stand upright without being bumped continually, and talked. For a large part of the journey a fair proportion of this time was during black-out hours and smoking was prohibited. It was the most uncomfortable period of an uncomfortable journey.

Later in the day it was possible to relax a little and play some bridge. In fact the rest of the day was spent in a rubber of bridge below and a breath of fresh air above. A short period on deck just before turning in was the pleasantest part of the day. The sea is always fascinating at night and when the phosphorescence picks out the tracery of the spray, it is almost fairyland again. One night in particular this phenomenon was most remarkable. It was possible to see the wakes of three or four boats nearest to us in the convoy, while ours was more brilliant than the Duchess's tiara.

We were all most eager to get home, but for some reason or other we had to put up at Oran for three days and it was there that we spent Christmas. The ship did extremely well for fare and it was a change to be able to take the usual Christmas walk even though it was only up and down the mole, and involved dodging the breakers as they came over the sea-wall. The Mediterranean was really rough that Christmas tide, far rougher than the Atlantic when we reached it, and later in the day, half the boat sported itself by watching poor unfortunates caught by these waves. Several were strong enough to carry fellows off the mole into the water with no serious results, happily - and one took a jeep in, while another completely smashed a wooden hut used by the A/A defences. The sea at least let us know that it was midwinter. But the Atlantic was just as peaceful, and eventually we saw the north coast of Ireland, and a day later the Clyde. Our welcome home was a marvellous scene of snow on the Scottish hills. Nothing could have been more appropriate after two years in the sun and sand of Africa and the rain of Italy.

Jack seems to have faded out of this story but he was there all the time and for "we" one might almost always read "Jack and I". He was certainly on the deck that morning as we saw the lowlands of Scotland. I hope he will be there in quite a lot more of my experiences, too.

A Brief Period in England

January - June 1994

We returned from the Middle East in January 1944 and were dumped in Norfolk, in Nissen huts among the Bryant and May forests between Thetford and Brandon. Norfolk is a lovely county, much under-rated generally, and it is no slight to it to say that there was deep resentment at being billeted in such a remote place and at such a time of year. Most of the regiment had been in the M.E. for two and a half years and I had been overseas for a year and ten months. The resentment was fuelled by the knowledge that some far less desert - scarred units than we were billeted on the south coast. I will not continue the passages from letters until I went abroad again, but I include a few quotations firstly in emphasis of the cold we felt.

"The weather has been most wretched. I don't really think I have felt warm once. There has been a biting wind and it has tried to snow on and off - it is at this moment. You can imagine what it is like underfoot."

"This morning there was snow on the ground and it has tried to snow all day. And to increase our discomfort we've got to go easy on the fuel. What we have got, has got to last a fortnight. So there will only be fires between 5 and 10 in the evening and hot water only two days a week. I know everyone is going to feel fuel rationing, but as you suggested, we are feeling the cold particularly as it's our first experience of anything but heat for two years. I don't know when I have ever felt as cold as during the last fortnight, and this afternoon and evening it has been worse than ever. The place is a quagmire so it's not possible or pleasant to take any exercise to get warm. The only thing is to sit in a top-coat, have periodic cups of tea in the Naafi, and then go to bed early."

However, in the Arctic winter of 1944, something did happen.

"On Thursday we had a parade for Monty - and we stood two and a half hours in the cold and sleet for him. After most elaborate dressing to get the lines straight, he altered everything when he came and told us to stand easy. 'He didn't want the men to stand to attention for him.' You know he is as good a playboy as soldier and he is a very good soldier. He made one of his usual speeches over a microphone. He wasn't too blatant in that, but he seemed absolutely confident that the war could 'be ended by the winter.' He attached terrific importance to the bombing, which he said had started already. He was quite caustic about the second front too. He didn't quite know which fronts we had been fighting on and was under the impression that there had been a spot of fighting in the past. Next week we have an inspection by Mr. and Mrs. X. We guess the King and Queen."

But there was no point in resentment. We had to make the best of the situation. We had leave. I was due for two weeks; that was all, after nearly two years abroad. We had half days, usually Saturdays, at King's Lynn or Cambridge or Newmarket. I managed two or three quick visits, apart from the leave, to home in Bedford, and I dashed up to London to meet my sister for a meal and a show. I saw "Arsenic and Old Lace" on one of these trips.

In almost every letter I mention going out for dinner, somewhere or other. There was a very pleasant hotel in Thetford and towards the end, we discovered the Great White Horse at Ipswich. I made the folks at home envious by telling them our menus; salmon, crab and lobster, for example. I also pointed out in one letter that the maximum price for a meal was 5/-.

We were equipped with a new British tank, the Cromwell, and took them to various ranges to test them and calibrate the guns, at Kirkcudbright, involving a very long and dismal train journey, and at Boyton and Blakeney, both in Norfolk and both with sand banks just off the coast on which the targets were put.

Eventually, three weeks before D-day, we went to Orwell Park, near Ipswich where we water-proofed the tanks and where we spent the period of strictest security of the thirty miles from the coast exclusion zone. From there we went to Felixstowe and loaded on to the tank landing craft, waiting for the day.

North West Europe

June 1994 - May 1945

16. 6. 44.

I am sorry I haven't written to you for, it must be, three weeks, but as you can imagine, there has been a good deal to do and little opportunity for writing. We were confined to camp in England a week or so before the invasion began. Then we went to the boat, sailed on Monday and arrived here late in the evening of "THE" day. We didn't land until the next afternoon. We got going pretty quickly and the days were long too - hence the little time. Reveille was about 4.30 and we were lucky if we got down before 1.30 the next morning. I have never felt fatigue much before. I was in a sort of stupor yesterday morning; I had trouble with my wireless set for two nights and it was after 3 when I had finished. The result was that I had 23 hours sleep between Monday night of last week and yesterday morning. But I think it has been worthwhile. We have been told that our work has upset Gerry's concentration and hence postponed any counter-attack for the moment. And of course every day is another day to build up our forces here, which must be quite considerable by this time. Once again I wish I was at home and could experience the excitement of waiting for the news; I'd rather have that sort of excitement than that of making the news.

I had a grandstand view of an R.A.F. night attack the other night - from about three miles off - and believe me, it was something to see. Each flare seemed to break into a hundred smaller ones until the whole area was most brilliantly lit up. Then the pathfinders laid the course and lastly, there was the rumble of bombs, no crumps at all.

19. 6. 44.

I must draw attention to my rise in rank. It has only come about through the loss to the regiment of some very good pals. I hope at least that some of them are P.O.W. Our big boss[*] is now major and squadron leader and a very good one he will make too. I am consequently his operator and the squadron wireless N.C.O., which carries two stripes with it. I have also to be the intelligence N.C.O. for the squadron (N.B. the "ce" not "t") and the other morning had to do a spot of quick mugging up of cipher.

Jack Cole was promoted yesterday too, which pleases me very much, as he has been in the regiment for over five years now and has had a bit of a raw deal, I think. He was on guard last night, but I think the occasion will call for a little celebration tonight if we can find anything to celebrate with. The only drink round here is cider, but we might be lucky and find someone going to the nearest town, who could bring back some Cognac or something.

We have been resting the last few days after quite a hectic time. Incidentally, we have seen a little of the Americans and I hope by this time the people at home have changed their opinion. They've been fighting magnificently. They made the progress which allowed us to do the breakthrough, which was our job on Tuesday and Wednesday. I think the most amazing thing about the fighting so far is how we have been able to retain the initiative, in this second stage, in spite of the main job being to build up the forces in the bridgehead. There have been counter-attacks, but of a local nature, and Gerry hasn't been able to concentrate for a large attack. Now, I believe, if it comes, we are strong enough to chew it into small pieces. And then will come the push. And what a push!

We are completely confident and I don't now give the war much of its sixth year.

One of our troops had an incredible story to tell of Tuesday. There were three Tigers, a most formidable German tank, and several Mark IV's in a town.[*] This troop went in to tackle them. They placed themselves and the infantry anti-tank guns so that the Germans were completely bottled up. Then they did some stalking and one by

---

[*]Captain Tony Jarvis.
[*]Villers Bocage.

one eliminated the Germans. One Mark IV shot by so quickly that our shots missed. A corporal shot out with his tank, fired at the rear of the Gerry, brewed it up and shot back, in reverse, before anyone knew what was happening. The last tank, a Tiger, took six hours to dispose of. He was bottled up in a road about 100 yards long. He attempted at one time to knock a house down with his H.E., and then by ramming, but he couldn't. In the end one of our sergeants shot a hole in a wall, so that he could get a cross view through the hole and a window into the street; then he sat and waited for the Tiger to come. The whole story is quite fantastic. We have been used to ranges of 2000 yards or more. Here it was about 10 yards.

Since getting back we have had quite a fuss made of us. Monty sent us a pack of cigarettes each. Then we had the American press correspondents about the place and yesterday they gave this regiment the honour of having the first Ensa show on the second front. I think we've earned it though, and in any case it is good for morale!

B.W.E.F. 26. 6. 44.

You will see we have a new address now. I suppose since it has been released that the Desert Rats are here, that we can have a new address.

All that you read about the Desert Rats, incidentally, and heard on the wireless from Frank Gillard, happened to us. We were told that he was broadcasting about us and so, of course, we listened. I expect by now you have pieced together what he said and what I said in my letter to you and connected us with the stories. We've been searching quite greedily in the papers for news of ourselves. I suppose what we did was spectacular and we came out in time for the correspondents to be down on us while the news was still red-hot. "The British are quite some race" - did you read that comment? The interview took place at the back of our tank.

We get papers quite regularly and not too old. There seem to be plenty of them, too - and every paper, excluding the Daily Worker! The division also issues a Jerboa Journal, a duplicated affair, which has the latest news in it. I imagine a good deal of this is from the news "at dictation speed" on the wireless, but quite obviously the news from the front is from other "well informed" sources.

The Monty policy of keeping the troops informed with what is going on has been pretty well maintained. We get to know fairly well what is happening. It means a good deal if you can see your own particular part in the larger picture.

I think the fall of Cherbourg should alter things greatly. Not that it is a large port, but now we have a fairly long line all facing one way. It is bound to effect the strategy. We still seem able to contain Gerry. I think quite definitely we still have the initiative and consequently, without bringing up large reinforcements, he can't concentrate for a counter-attack. I hope we are ready for our drive before he can concentrate.

The weather has not been at all what it might have been. Yesterday it rained most of the day and last night was wettish too. Today has been stormy, much more like April. There was some very heavy rain this afternoon, but fortunately we can get the bivvy up and keep dry.

3. 7. 44.

I'm sorry there was such a gap in my correspondence to you, but I'm afraid it was inevitable. Still, now you've had one since our biggest duffy and I hope your anxiety has quietened a bit.

I didn't have to use pep tablets this time. We carry them in case of emergency and if we'd gone on an hour longer, I should have had to have taken them. I was to a certain extent unlucky. I had trouble with my set on two days and consequently had to change it at night, which meant the possible three hours' sleep was cut down to one hour one night and forty minutes the next. When we got back, at 5 o'clock in the morning, I unrolled my bed and must just have collapsed on it, as I woke up an hour or so later feeling chilly.

The real trouble about this tiredness is that the days are so long. I suppose there are only four or five hours of real darkness and by the time all the necessary is done, this is cut down to three and a half to four hours' sleeping. We've been lucky in not having to keep this up for too long at a stretch.

The old Monty custom of keeping the troops informed is going well. We get a resume of the battle front, usually one a day, and this afternoon we have had a visit from the divisional education officer who has given us a much wider picture. He is very optimistic. He says we have now accomplished the first three tasks - made a landing, extended the bridgehead to a sizeable area and captured a port - and the fourth has begun and will soon proceed apace; the smashing of the German army in France. We, Jack Cole and I, have just been to see an old school pal of his, who is now in the H.Q. of a neighbouring division. He said that it is the general view that there will be one battle and one battle only in France and that is the one developing now.

You know if you look at the moves on a fair scaled map, the manoeuvres are exactly like the old history book battles of Agincourt or Blenheim or somewhere, except that the battlefield extends for about a hundred miles instead of a couple of dozen acres and the time is measured in weeks instead of hours. But really though, the principles are the same.

I saw a couple of prisoners up there, that had just been brought in. You never saw anything more resembling scarecrows in your life.

They must have been in the line days on days. They had their camouflage ground sheets on too, and these and their clothes were all tattered and torn. Incidentally, the only Germans I've spoken to over here are Alsatians.

I think that what is put in the papers is essentially true, although it is camouflaged in a good deal of journalese. I don't think there have been many overstatements that I've spotted. Perhaps the correspondents learnt their lesson in Africa.

Did you hear the despatch on the Villers Bocage R.A.F. raid the other night? We saw that raid and when we first spotted the bombers coming, we could hardly believe our eyes. They were not in close Yankee formation for one thing, and eventually they just strung out from one side of the horizon to the other. I've read in the papers about aeroplanes swarming like flies, but I didn't realise what they meant until I saw these. They were exactly like flies in the desert. Then they just wheeled in over the target and terrific clouds of smoke and dust came up. 12 minutes was the official time for the 1300 tons, I believe, and it certainly did not seem as long to us.

I believe the B.B.C. news have said three planes were lost, but I saw only two come down. Villers must be a complete wreck now - two houses standing, isn't it? A fair bit of the place was burning when we left it.

7. 7. 44.

Forgive any dirty finger marks on the letter. I've just put the evening meal on, and the pots are not as clean on the outside as they might be. It's going to be steak tonight, heated up in the tins, "vegetable macedoine" it says on the tins, which we will mash up and fry, and date pudding, also in a tin. Our rations are not bad and at least are easy to cook, as nearly everything just needs heating up in the tins. I think I appreciate puddings as much as anything; marmalade, treacle, date, sultana and even rice. Then occasionally there are tins of fruit.

Our little celebration didn't materialise. We have in point of fact been extremely temperate since getting here, just a little cider a fortnight ago, which was not good cider by any means, and last night for the first time - and as far as I am concerned, the last time - a glass of Calvados at a local estaminet. Jack and I went down there to sample things and found the local liqueur, an apple brandy and almost pure alcohol. I believe it is inadvisable to smoke for some little time after it! Anyhow one small glass was sufficient.

Our one piece of excitement here today was to see a Messerschmidt brought down. Actually, he fell at the closest quarters I've been to one. A/A took part of a wing off and he lost control, span down and fell in a field three hundred yards away. I'm not bloodthirsty, but it was good to see the German cross on the wing spinning round and round.

Last night we walked up to see a German tank that had been brought in almost intact. It really does look as if there is something in his shortage of petrol. I don't believe for one minute that he hasn't supplies somewhere, but I think that the Air Force is making it increasingly difficult for him to get it to the right place at the right time. The tank looked a runner, but all the leads to the plugs were cut; so presumably he had to immobilise it.

23. 7. 44.

I've just heard that this squadron has four decorations for the Villers episode - one D.S.O., one M.C., one M.M., and one D.C.M., which is not bad going for one squadron, is it? There is another M.C. in another squadron.

I can't tell you very much about the last affair. The only incident that will interest you now was when we took four prisoners. I felt a biff on my head and the Major gave me his revolver saying, "Cover me." There were a couple of Gerries who had come out of some corn, (we were just on the edge of a cornfield) and given themselves up. We asked if there were any more, and one turned round and shouted, "Karl," and Karl came out also. Then I spotted a fourth, crouching down in a hole on the edge of the cornfield. We called him in too, and what a poor pathetic looking fellow he was, not more than 18, if he was that, and weeping. Two were Poles and two Germans. I think the younger ones expected to be shot at any moment, but they were quite reassured, I believe, by the time we had handed them over. It's a very trifling incident but it confirms some of what you might read in the papers.

A monk had just wandered across the orchard. There is an Abbey quite near, knocked about a bit now. I should imagine that both sides have considered that the dome is a good observation point. The folk at the farm are devout Catholics. We see them toddle off in their Sunday best several times a week and I suppose the monk in his flowing white is returning the compliment.

10. 8. 44.

There is no more news I can tell you from this end, but that is not necessarily because nothing is happening. We are in very pleasant country again, at the moment in a valley, with a small stream running at the bottom and hay fields rising at each side. The hay in this field has been half cut; I should imagine it was in that state when the battle came this way. Still, it is very pleasant as it is. I hope the crops will not be wasted. Round Caen the wheat looked ready to reap, but there was little opportunity to do that. A certain amount of the cattle is being killed too, but not a lot really, and what is left looks healthy enough. It should help to feed France.

A calf was born in the corner of the field where we were the other day. It was interesting to watch the youngster. After about ten minutes it rose to its legs rather shakily and toddled off for a drink. He spent the next hour in this pleasant occupation.

August 18th/19th. The Falaise gap was closed.

20. 8. 44.

I don't know how I shall spend tomorrow. We never know one day to the next - nor really one hour to the next. This morning I've had a real good wash-day, first myself and then the clothes. The sun has come out quite strongly and so I'm hoping to get things dry before we have to move on.

You can imagine we have been pretty busy recently. I suppose the stage of the campaign has been reached when every single formation is needed to keep Gerry on the move. We've come across quite a number of prisoners this week, and they seem a poor lot. Most of them complain of having had no food for three days. A couple of French people found their way through to us from a nearby village yesterday to tell us that a few Germans were there - 25 they said, and they began pillaging the houses, particularly for food. Of course, practically all the houses were deserted. I've often wondered who turned the places upside down so much, with the drawers turned out, crockery all over the place and so on. I couldn't really believe that our fellows looted to this extent, and it seems confirmed Gerry does it just before he leaves.

Of course I believe the average German would pack it in if he knew what was happening behind him, but he doesn't seem to know what is happening a thousand yards ahead, let alone 70 miles to his rear. The picture of the battle has changed completely this week, hasn't it? I hope all the army this side of the Seine can be disposed of. The R.A.F. seems to be doing a good deal towards this. We are certainly beginning to see a good deal of destroyed equipment of various kinds along the roads.

27 8. 44.

Did the weather brighten up last week after a bad beginning? It has not been too bad since Tuesday and the last day or two has been really warm. It's just the sort of weather the R.A.F. wants. I understand the weather last week-end which was bad, helped us in the long run as Gerry got stuck and couldn't beat a hasty retreat as he otherwise might have done.

We have seen some of the R.A.F. destruction this week - it is almost incredible. I will believe anything I read in the papers or hear on the wireless now. I've seen miles of road strewn with trucks of all descriptions, tanks, guns and horse drawn carts, with the horses, and I believe this road was nothing compared with others. And not only the roads. There was hardly a field alongside the road without at least one vehicle along the hedge or in a corner that had been "brewed up". The rocket seems a very much better aerial weapon than the bomb - it's so much more accurate. I could half imagine what the panic must have been like. The horses would just bolt, of course, and the men would be much like the horses. I hope now there will be another good kill at the Seine - then perhaps the Somme and so on. Who knows?

No, I know no more than you; in fact we rely on the B.B.C. news for our information largely. Just occasionally we get some from official sources, but everyone is very close with information these days. Quite rightly, as it is perfectly obvious Gerry doesn't know what was going on a couple of miles away, let alone 50. His communications had been cut to that extent. Of course I think we did not get as depressed as some people did, at the slowness of things up to three weeks ago. It was obvious that there had got to be an out-flanking movement and that this had to be angled for. Also, it has always been Monty's plan to have the battle first - destroy armies, then conquer territories. That is what happened out here again. It seems Gerry is going to have a job to stabilise himself anywhere now, certainly not on the Seine. He's lost so much infantry and equipment.

I forget if I told you that we had some good news about one of the fellows we thought killed at Villers Bocage. He was taken prisoner and has now been recaptured by the Americans and is back in England. I've heard this morning that the fellow whose return to the regiment we celebrated at Ipswich and whom I mentioned before, has got back in the same way. It's quite amazing to us.

August 28th, the Seine crossed.
September 2nd, the Somme crossed.
September 8th, arrived in Antwerp.

B.L.A. 9. 9. 44.

I managed to get a note off the other day, but it was only a few minutes before we had a bit of excitement - nothing dangerous, just some Gerries trying to get away and driving hell for leather right into our arms. I don't know who was more surprised - they or we.

I think we must have had the kill at Falaise. There was very little on the Seine and not very much more on the Somme. To show how disorganised they were, we found three "88" guns just over the river. You know the "88" is a very formidable gun, one of the best in the world. This battery could easily have covered the bridge and prevented all crossing, but when we saw them some 2000 yards away, they were firing in the other direction and didn't take too long to immobilise. Quite near there were six that had been destroyed and then abandoned.

After that it really was just a matter of collecting the prisoners, or bringing them into the frame of mind to surrender and then finding someone to look after them. I suppose our bag - the regiment's - was 500-600 a day. We couldn't have done this except for the patriots. They really are amazing! They are well organised and the White Brigade in Belgium has been fully trained, underground of course. Now it is a fighting body and not just guerrillas. I think the loveliest sight was a real greybeard, sitting on top of a tombstone in a village, manning a captured automatic gun. And the most ironic thing; a couple of days ago, we took 250 prisoners, took their arms from them, gave them to the patriots and let them lead them away.

The reception we have had has been terrific, flags and waving crowds for mile after mile. Here, only this afternoon, we were invited to an estaminet, given beer and cigars, and even a special bottle was produced (of gin), from a backroom and we were not allowed to pay for anything. We are in the centre of a square where every other building is an estaminet. I counted fifteen just now. The only trouble is that the Gerry rate of exchange is against us and it is too soon for the Belgian Government to have organised down to this detail.

The people want to talk too. Every single one who passes, smiles or speaks or winks. We have heard numerous tales too, of an Englishman who has not been out of the same building for four years, but has not been seen since Monday afternoon! And of radios hidden away all this time but somehow or other used for the B.B.C. news. Everyone says how they used to listen to this to know how the war was going, of the flags coming out before the Gerry left and how he fled underneath them, and a hundred and one other tales too.

One I must tell you though. This fellow had been transported to work in Germany and escaped twice. He showed us a letter, just a blank piece of paper, that he would have sent to his wife if he had been caught a third time. On the back was his address, but with both Brussels and Antwerp on it. If he had been caught near Brussels, he would have crossed Antwerp out and vice versa. But the point of the story is that the workshop in Germany had to turn out 500 of a certain thing a day, but 400 of them were always useless. The foreman used to say, "If you do bad work like this, Germany will never win the war." To which they replied, "We don't mind." And as he walked away, he said, "Nor do I. I'm a Communist."

We've not had a great deal of loot; the withdrawal was too orderly or too well destroyed by the R.A.F, but we found a dozen bottles of Benedictine (genuine stuff) at the "88" place on Sunday.

19. 9. 44.

Yes, we are hoping that this war in the west will end quickly now. That dash across France and Belgium must have been at least up to schedule, if not in front. I think the high Command must have allowed for, if not anticipated, a stand somewhere, on the Seine or the Somme. I see Hanner Swaffer in one of the papers suggests that we are a fortnight before schedule, which would just about account for a set-piece attack on some defences. I don't fancy a winter campaign in these parts - and still less, I think, the job of sitting down and waiting for spring before we can attack. If the thing is not finished in a month though, I suppose that is what will happen.

I have seen several French or Belgian children in red, white and blue, or red, black and yellow frocks and apparently the idea has reached England too. I hope all this is not counting chickens before they are hatched, although it is difficult to see how Germany can avoid being defeated now. In any case, is there going to be an Armistice Day? Or will Germany just go on resisting until the whole country is occupied and the war fizzles out like that? Personally I don't think it will, but that is a minority opinion among the fellows here. There must come a point when the Army, the people and even the Nazis see that to resist any more would mean the useless sacrifice of civilian lives and property. I want to know when that point will be reached. Believe me, the country in Germany is going to suffer. We are not going to pull reins because there are civilians about. If a village stands in the way, then the artillery will obliterate it. We shall not try other means first as we have up to now. Perhaps in the long run it will be better for the Germans to experience war like this.

29. 9. 44.

We had a very good time last week-end, but unfortunately under these conditions just as we get dug in, we have to undig ourselves again. At the moment we are at a farm, which reminded me at the moment I saw it of the house at Hayes. I can see why it is called a Dutch house now. It is nothing like it really. There is a cowshed and other farm buildings all under the same roof. We are actually sleeping in the cowshed, but I think it must have been well cleaned out before we arrived and fresh straw put down as it is very clean now and comfortable. It is very much better than sleeping out in a tent in this Autumn weather. Last night for example, at 5 o'clock there was a heavy ground mist rising.

The people seemed a little suspicious for the first 24 hours we were here. I don't know whether they expected us to be like the Gerries, but gradually they thawed. The farmer, a tall, spare and very dour fellow, now has plenty of smiles. There are numerous young folk and cats and dogs, and so of course we get on very well. I suppose it is a bit of a change for these people who have been used to Gerry for four years, and they cannot acclimatise themselves rapidly in the first half-hour.

About the hair-cropping; there have been numerous articles and letters in the papers, calling this kind of thing barbaric and so on. I think I remember A.J. Cummings saying it must be stopped. But to my mind that is just one more piece of evidence that the people at home have no conception of what they missed by the skin of their teeth in 1940. I think the authorities have retained amazing control. It couldn't have been easy in the extremely fluid state of affairs that existed, and to some measure, still exists. But we have certainly seen no demonstrations - only those of welcome to us. This morning we've had two eggs for breakfast, the gift of the Dutch people. I think it was a bit silly of the French government to try to dissolve the F.F.I. After all, they played a major part in the liberation of France and naturally have some pride in their arms now. The obvious thing was to incorporate them, which has been done now and should have been done first.

The demobilisation plans seem to me to be very fair indeed. I'm afraid a lot of these reforms are vote catching - increases in pay and the open neck, collar and tie business. They have been five years before they could do these things and it seems rather suspicious that they have made their minds up now that an election is in sight. But I don't think there will be many soldiers with votes. We can't get hold of the forms which we have to fill up. There were notices about it before we left England. Both then and several times since I've tried to get one, but without success. I'm going to have another go however. Once again, to quote the correspondence columns of the newspapers, it seems a general state of affairs. I have never spoken to any soldier who has seen one of these forms.

We have had mushrooms quite recently, although we seem to have passed through the right part of the country now. They made a very welcome addition to the menu, particularly as the rations aren't very bright at the moment. Rather more than half now are captured German rations and I can sympathise with the German soldier. The jam, (so called), is in wooden boxes and comes out in a lump. It is obviously mashed swede, with a synthetic taste. About the only good thing are the vegetables, which have been processed somehow, but still remain fresh. We've had peas, runner beans and spinach like this and they have all been good.

15. 10. 44.

I have at last managed to get Army Form B 2626, or in other words, the voting by proxy form. I think I told you that I had made another attempt to get one. Nothing happened through that, but a couple of nights ago, the Major was talking about it and I told him I had asked six times now. Whether he put some dynamite behind someone or not, I don't know, but the forms turned up this morning. I feel I have accomplished something at last, after eight months of trying. The pictures of those Dutch children before the war were taken at Middleburg. We went right round Walcheren. I remember standing on the enormous sea wall at Westcapelle, which has now been broken in. Lord knows what bombs they used to break it, as the granite blocks of which it was built weighed ten tons each and there was a slope of about a hundred yards of these showing at low tide. We crossed from the mainland from Bressing to Flushing, both of which are very much in the news now.

I've seen practically nothing of the places I've seen before though - just Antwerp, and when we left, we came through Malines. I've been through that from Brussels to Antwerp by train and seen the famous bell tower from the carriage. This time we passed quite close to the cathedral. There is a marvellous Guild Hall there too - all that these old Flemish medieval Guild Halls should be. I didn't see much of Antwerp that I hadn't seen before though. The manager of Fords took me round for an hour or so in his car, but the cathedral was locked and in any case, the famous Rubens pictures inside had been removed. He did take me to Rubens house though, which I didn't see before and it was most interesting. One wing was built in Flemish style and one in Italian. Once again though, all the pictures and cartoons which were normally there, were right away in cellars somewhere. It was a lovely afternoon and not raining as it was in 1933, (I believe) and so I had a much better impression of the city. Most of the things which this fellow wanted to show me, were such places as the headquarters of the Gestapo or their gaol, (an ordinary house), and things of that description.

22. 10. 44.

I don't think the weather is any better than yours. Yours certainly must feel very lousy if it is. We had several days of biting cold but fairly dry; then last night it began to rain and today it has been misty, although warmer. When it does dry, the ground dries up pretty quickly. I've been surprised at how sandy the land is everywhere, the seaside variety of sand too. There is very little top soil and the sand is all over the country as far as I can see.

At the moment we are in a pub, or the equivalent of one. The bar place we have turned into a canteen, the proprietor doing his best to find beer for us, and we are sleeping upstairs. It's a house shaped like yours, but the absurd part is that all the first floor is really open, with lath and plaster partitions put along two sides to form very small rooms. The bulk of it is a large landing and apparently useless, except as a lumber room; I believe it is quite common in house construction here.

This seems to be a most devout village and there is quite a crowd at the service each morning. This morning, though, everyone must have been there. It looked as if they were coming out of a football match at the end.

We've been busy the last few days again, liberating a place or two on our way. It was really strange how the front became fluid again last week. It shows that we have still very much retained an offensive spirit in spite of what some of the newspapers are saying. I think there must be nibbling going on all the time.

7. 11. 44.

We've left the pub some time ago now and at the moment are ensconced in a farm. We are sleeping in the barn and have a good deal of straw on the floor which makes it nice and warm. We've got a lean-to outside under which we cook. There is an incredible number of people in the house - 27, I think it is, as there are bits and pieces of another family evacuated and who have come here. All the whole lot are most devout and troop off to church regularly every morning. Two or three fellows of about 20 years old in the party speak a little English and like to get into conversation. They love it if we will go in at nights. But the canteen has been popular the last few nights. We've managed to get a little "hooch" and consequently the farm people haven't seen much of us at nights.

I don't know how really devout these folk are. It might almost seem an excuse for a holiday. Last week they all had two days holiday, for All Souls Day and All Saints Day, and today it is another because it is the day of the Patron Saint. They are all trooping off now again - 3.30 in the afternoon. I've never seen such people for going to church and I'm told inside the church it is quite a sight. All the women still sit on one side and all the men on the other.

Jack Cole is dug into a house which is insisting on doing all the cooking for them. Last night I went up and the lady of the house was making the most enormous pancakes for them; the chap up there is some sort of an overseer on the farms about here. Once again their devotion shows. The "parlour" is littered with effigies and statues - most inappropriate to my mind in a room where there is smoking and mild gambling going on.

I'm due to go into the nearest big town tomorrow to see Emlyn Williams in "Blithe Spirit". Ensa and the stars certainly seem willing to come forward and not remain in Brussels or Paris or other base areas as they did rather in N. Africa.

On Sunday we had a football match against the local team. It was billed all over the place as a "Grand Sporting Event" and although there was a high wind, it was quite enjoyable to watch. There was a crowd too, but we managed to maintain the sporting record of the British by winning 2-1. That was not a bad achievement as it was only a squadron team.

17. 11. 44.

I was having two days' leave in Brussels this time last week. The Belgians apparently give their children toys on Dec. 6th., St. Nicholas day. I realise for the first time what Santa Claus means now. The shops had enormous displays of toys which well compared with the pre-war set-outs at Gamages and the like, so much for shortages in occupied countries. I spent one morning looking at the shops and decided that I would see all before I bought Stephen anything. Then as usual in the continental way, they had taken the occasion of Armistice Day last Saturday to have a general holiday and so I couldn't buy anything.

The weather is still very cold. It has been a biting wind that has caused the trouble. I have told you about our Zute suits and you will have read about them in the papers by now. We have been glad of them these last three days. They at least keep the wind out. We've been huddled round huge fires. We were in a wood of pine trees yesterday which became thinner and thinner as the day proceeded.

I dare say you've seen a good deal about the flame throwers in the papers recently. I saw them for the first time in action the other night and it was a most fantastic sight. It reminded me more of a Walt Disney film than anything else, just a black background with these jets of brilliant colour darting out. I don't think I would like to be on the receiving end of it. I don't think I should wait for it to get me. I'd roll over and die of fright to begin with.

8. 12. 44.

I'm afraid this letter will be rather disjointed. I'm writing it in the living room and the lady of the house has been trying to explain to me the troubles of evacuation. She comes from Utrecht really and her Dutch is more difficult to understand than that of people we have met before. Anyhow, I take it there are five hundred evacuees coming into the village and she has been expressing the same opinions as were expressed in England at the beginning of the war. They come from farms, and are half-wits; they smell, have enormous families and all the rest of it. Anyhow, having thirteen soldiers in the house should exempt her, I should think.

Then the lad of the house is in none too pleasant a mood at the moment. He is usually a happy little kid, but he had no afternoon nap today. He was most excited yesterday morning - St. Nicholas Day - when he had his presents and dragged me into the room to see them. The kids all get very thrilled by it here and they do the job properly, with Father Christmas, or rather St. Nicholas, who is accompanied by a black page, Black Peter. That bit of the legend sounds like Wenceslas to me.

Yesterday I had the afternoon off and managed to see a play and a film [*]. The play was "A Soldier for Christmas", with Joyce Barbour and Richard Beatty from Wyndhams. I enjoyed the chance of seeing a real live show again. It's pretty good to see a play with first class people in it. The film was another version of "The Bridge at San Luis Rey". This version is good for those who haven't read the book or seen the previous film. It certainly does not keep the atmosphere of the book, which I think is a little masterpiece.

I would have been quite content to see the play by myself, but one has to fill the time in somehow. Hence two shows in one day. I really do feel that Toc H or someone should open up clubs, rest rooms or call them what you will in places like these, as no soldier wants to tramp the streets.

That picture in the News Chronicle is the Zute suit all right. They have been very useful, but they are better to keep the wind out than the rain. They will turn a shower but they won't stand twelve hours of continuous rain and we've had that. Still, I am grateful for mine.

---

[*] In Eindhoven.

I didn't like wearing a greatcoat in the tank. It got creased for one thing, and also, I used to rip all the buttons off the back and they are almost impossible to replace now.

26. 12. 44.

The fellows here have been saying for a long time, "I'm Dreaming of a White Christmas," and they've got one this year, not with snow but with frost. But thank heavens, it isn't raining. I've just done the smalls and put them out on the line. I fully expect to bring them in in an hour or so as hard as boards, but they'll get the fresh air for a bit. So far this has been the best Christmas Eve, with a bit of binge in the billet. That of course has made all the difference being in a civilian house. We managed to get hold of some cognac and did it rather more than justice. We'd put three to bed by 8 o'clock! The man of the house was pretty rough yesterday too. He and another fellow both made Christmas dinner of three aspirins. But I don't suppose - I hope not anyway - that we shall have another Christmas under these circumstances, and therefore I think a little celebration was well justified. The Dutch of course haven't seen any good cognac for four years.

We had a very good dinner yesterday; the army tinned turkey helped out with some pork, Christmas pudding and mince pies. Then an informal - or spontaneous - sing-song afterwards, very much better than if something had been organised.

Last night we spent quietly in here, just playing cards, and reading. I thought of you all a number of times and tried to imagine what you were doing. While we were sitting round the stove - the Kakle, or something like that - I thought of you round the fire at home, probably listening to the same programme on the wireless too. But we had something you wouldn't have had - apple flaps - which are Dutch fare on Christmas day, apparently. They are rings of apple, dipped in batter and fried, so that they turn out like drop-scones with a round of apple in them and they are very nice. There was also "Tart" last night, really like the continental cakes we've enjoyed so much, a big round sandwich cake with whirled cream on it.

14. 1. 45.

Just a very short note to let you know that as far as I know at the moment, I shall be coming on leave next week-end. My D-day, which means the travelling day at the beginning, is next Saturday. The snag is that if something should crop up in between, I couldn't let you know. Anyhow, that is the situation.

6. 3. 45.

Heaven alone knows how long it is since I wrote to you. You will have heard by now that I have been on hors de combat for a week, and as the combat was a trifle sticky, from that point of view I don't mind. The burns I got were very superficial; I didn't stay long enough to get sizzled and two or three good coats of grease put things right. The rest, too, seems to have stopped any shock, which was the real reason I was evacuated, I think. Anyhow I am quite all right again now, at the convalescent depot, and I hope to be away from here after the week-end. Then there is a weary trek back to the regiment. I haven't the slightest idea how long this will take, but it will be a fortnight at least. And in all this time I'll get no mail.

The worst thing about all this is that I've lost almost everything. The tank just went straight up in flames and there was only one reaction - bail out. It's a very good thing we did not stop to retrieve anything as it was hit again as we got out of the top and on to the ground. The beds were already burning when I got out of the turret and so I doubt if we could have saved anything. I keep thinking of all the small things I have lost - books, flints, mirror and so on. I don't think I shall ever collect as much together again. The one thing that I really regret is the writing case the staff gave me when I left Ewhurst. It has been a great boon and that is why I carried it round with me although there has been the possibility of this happening of course.

One result of being in back areas is that I saw an Ensa show on Saturday at the hospital and a film last night. I was kept in the convalescent depot to help on as education staff.

12. Br. Con. Depot.* 25. 4. 45.

I've been quite enjoying the work here this week. There is not a lot of it and the groups not really large - sometimes 25-30, occasionally 50-60. The fellows all seem anxious to listen but it's quite difficult to get them to talk and as I see it, half the point of the Army Education is to get them to talk and express themselves.

I more than ever believe the thing we've discussed over and over again. A fellow can't express himself because he's not thinking clearly and when he's got to the point of marshalling his thoughts, then the words will flow all right. The curriculum is almost entirely what we should have called "civics" at school. Some of last week's topics were housing, health, town planning with a quiz and a Brains Trust thrown in and a weekly news summary.

I believe we are gradually changing this Toc H club here. The Warden showed me a circular from Tubby and it would seem that it is quite general for these places to develop into little but canteens. It is a great pity but where there is no canteen, I suppose it is necessary work. But apart from that, the only things the place runs during the week are a whist drive and a dance. That should surely not be.

The news the last two days has been very good again, hasn't it? I'm so glad they have tackled the Rhine, without too long a pause after the last offensive and so not given him much of a chance to re-organise. I don't see how he can have a lot on the other side, but some of what there is will be tough. Their first Parachute Army is very determined, I know from personal experience. I can't quite see when they will decide to give up. It must be quite obvious to them that they haven't got a chance but at what point will this lead them to lay down their weapons? The longer they fight, the more the country is going to suffer. Surely the end can't be very far off now.

The weather certainly has been grand the last week and all in our favour. This morning it is a little cloudy but the clouds are obviously light and high and so I hope it will not interfere with support for the Army. Yesterday we saw plenty of heavies coming back, and what a marvellous sight they looked in the sun! It's a horrible thought when you consider what they have just done. We were discussing the other night how decent, ordinary fellows can create so much destruction and

---

*At Den Hahn, or Le Coq sur Mer.

come to the conclusion it was because in modern war one didn't immediately see the result of one's bombing. It's a distant, impersonal sort of destruction.

POSTSCRIPT

When the war ended, I was still at the convalescent depot. On June 6th, the first anniversary of D-day, the army were excused all parades and duties, as its way of saying that the troops had a holiday. I went to Bruges where I spent a typical sight-seeing day, renewing memories of my first trip abroad in 1932. When I returned, I was told that a lieutenant from the regiment had been for me to take me back. By V.E. day, it had reached Hamburg and was in private houses in Blankenese on the Elbe. Our journey in a 15 cwt. truck took us through the Ruhr and some of the most heavily bombed areas. The Dortmund-Ems canal, mention of which we had heard so many times in R.A.F bulletins, was empty and a way in bull-dozed down the bank, across the bed and up the other side, in place of a bridge, all presumably having been destroyed. At Düsseldorf, passing the railway station I saw a large locomotive standing upright on its tender and wondered what sort of force had lifted such a tonnage into that position. Hanover was a city of burnt-out houses. Of Hamburg it was said that 96% of the buildings had suffered some damage. One huge concrete air-raid shelter, several storeys high, had a rent from top to bottom and I knew then what "block-buster" meant. At the end of the journey I realised that great as the damage was in London, it was not comparable with that of these German cities. And along all roads through the countryside were files of refugees trailing their belongings on little hand-carts and trolleys.

The morning after I reached the regiment, the colonel told me that I had been brought back to run the Army Education Scheme in the regiment. I was promoted to sergeant and excused all parades and duties. But it was a challenge for which I was very grateful. The H.Q. Squadron was in a schloss at Lehmkuhlen, between Hamburg and Lübeck, and there was plenty of room for classrooms and workshops. But the biggest advantage was the quality of the personnel. The regiment had entered the war as a territorial unit and somehow, with all the changes that had necessarily happened and all the new arrivals as reinforcements from time to time, both in the desert and in Europe, it had retained that territorial atmosphere and the intellectual quality of the men.

Eventually I managed to get some thirty subjects covered from languages, French, German, Italian, through pure, basic English, to Economics and Law and then the practical occupations, carpentry and snobbing. The regiment was still operational and it was difficult to maintain any consistent courses, but the classes that took place provided a stimulus beyond just recreational pastimes.

There was one experience which I have thought of many times since when there has been the usual uninformed criticism of modern practice and standards in schools in the post-war years. Our regimental educational scheme found favour with the brigade and the Colonel in charge there sent the Captain of a pioneer group to see what we were doing. He had sixty men building an air-strip a few miles away. After I had shown him the plan and some of the classes in operation that morning, he looked at me with tears in his eyes and said,

"How can I possibly do this? Forty of my men can't read."

All I could possibly do was to advise him to get the twenty who could to teach the forty who couldn't.

Then in October came the news that I was due for a class B release, as a schoolmaster, and after a 42 hour train journey I eventually arrived back at Catterick, where I had begun, for the process of getting out of the Army. I had three weeks' leave, all I was due for on a Class B release, and returned to the classroom for exactly a month before Christmas 1945.

And was it all worthwhile? I can honestly say now that I did not then and have not since felt any regrets.

Up to 1938 I could have been a pacifist and conscientious objector, but events in Austria and Czechoslovakia convinced me and many like me that a stand had to be made, whatever the consequences. Nazism and its practices had to be stopped. I say "whatever the consequences". I came through more or less unscathed but there were many who did not, the five in the tank in front of us, when I bailed out for the last time and the war ended for me, for example. There were times when I did not think I would come through the next ten minutes, at Alamein or Villers Bocage, to cite two places. But I did and I am thankful for the experience. On the most mundane level, I am thankful for having seen some of the world, Table Mountain, the Pyramids, Leptis Magna, as well as the way people live.

I hope that sharing these experiences will be of interest to those who have had like experiences. I especially hope that those who are lucky enough to be too young to have had them (or are they?) will be able to get some of the feel of them through this book.